I Almost Lost Her

A Memoir of Unthinkable Tragedy

André Xavier

To continue to follow Charlie's recovery please visit :

www.cheeringoncharlie.com

TABLE OF CONTENTS

"I am praying that God gives me the strength to fulfill this new role that He has assigned to me. I accept it. I just don't know how I am going to do it."

—Excerpt From Journal Entry September 11, 2021

CHAPTER 1

In A Flash

Charlie rubbed her neck, nodding as I spoke.

"See? You're in so much pain you can barely stand still. You can't go to work tomorrow—you need to stay here, take care of yourself, and go to the chiropractor."

"I just need to finish this one project, André," she replied, letting go of her neck.

Charlie had spent the last week working to make things perfect for a friends and family night we were hosting at the brewery, Patch, we'd purchased and planned to re-open in a few weeks-time. She'd been sanding and staining various things, but her last project had her staring down at the frame of a large chalk board business partner, Jon's father had made. The chalk board would sit in the kids' area. Although she was typically in charge of marketing for our businesses, Charlie had been there every day—more than I liked—doing manual labor, working with contractors, and helping Jon get things ready. She'd prioritized that work over her own well-being.

As she reached for her neck again, white hot frustration rose from my core. I took a breath and responded slowly, carefully annunciating each word, "You've been there far too much. It's dinner time now and you're only just getting home. You're never here early enough to help this week. You're spending every moment at the brewery and barely any time here with the boys or doing anything else. Why are you bothering to do all this? Nobody cares what you do, it doesn't matter. We have people to. . ."

She cut me off, "I'm there because you're *not* there. Someone needs to be there helping Jon—this is a partnership."

"Charlie, let me be clear. Jon knows that my partnership is not about doing handywork; I'm not a handy person. My role is to secure funding and manage the money. That's my skill—being the finance person."

"Right," she responded, "I understand, but Jon's parents and fiancé have been helping on and off for months. Now we're days from opening and it's all-hands-on-deck. If you can't help, then at least I should." She stared at me with tired eyes, her blond hair pulled back in a ponytail flecked with bits of sawdust. She winced as she rubbed her neck harder.

"Listen, no one asked you to do this. You gave yourself this job and you're injuring yourself. I don't understand it." Just as I paused to gather my thoughts, my mom, who was staying with us at the time, walked into the kitchen. She looked at me as if to ask what was going on. I translated briefly in Portuguese what we'd been discussing.

My mom looked at Charlie and said in her signature sweet and caring tone, "You're in so much pain, honey. You really should give yourself some rest. We just want you to take care of yourself so you don't get more injured. Can you skip tomorrow?"

Charlie's face turned red as she closed her eyes as if to compose herself. She drew a breath and responded, "I can't. The paint needs time to cure, so if I don't go, it won't be ready in time and—"

"You know what, Charlie?" I interrupted, "Whatever. Just do what you want."

Charlie didn't respond—she was in a fight she knew she couldn't win. It was a fight with an entity she'd been fighting for twelve years and would likely fight for the rest of her life: my ego.

The next day I woke to the sound of birds chirping outside our window. A crack in the curtains illuminated Charlie's empty spot in the bed. She'd gone to work. I wasn't even surprised. Charlie was strong-willed. She wouldn't let an argument between us stop her from doing the work she felt responsible for.

I checked my email on my phone before getting out of bed as my mom tended to the boys. I was showered and ready to head out to do some errands around 8:30 when I realized I didn't have my car keys. I searched everywhere for them—first the obvious places like tabletops and drawers—then in less obvious places like under beds and in our hamper. Remembering that Charlie had driven my car the day before, I had a feeling she'd accidentally taken them with her, which added a stinging quality to my irritation. I'd asked her not to leave today. She needed a break. She needed to take care of herself. She needed to take care of us.

I grabbed my phone, scrolled to Charlie's name and tapped it. I pushed my coffee cup out of the way as I leaned forward on the granite countertop, which was cold on my elbows.

"Hey," Charlie answered after three rings.

"Charlie, I'm trying to leave and I don't have my keys."

There was rustling in the background.

"Do you have them?" I asked.

"Please don't kill me," she responded. "I do have them."

I knew it.

"Charlie," I said, rubbing my brow. "I should make you get into your car right now and drive them to me."

"Please don't," she begged. "I won't be too much longer, I'm so close to finishing this project and I have a chiropractor appointment at three."

"Okay fine," I replied, easing my tone, happy that she'd at least made an appointment with the chiropractor. "I'll see you later today."

"I love you," she said.

"Love you too," I said, flatly.

I hung up the phone.

Satisfied that Charlie would be home early and would finally prioritize her wellbeing, I was able to put my frustration aside and get to work. I responded to emails, spoke to potential investors, and talked to other key players on our team.

An hour later, my phone rang. Charlie was on the other end. Her breath was heavy. "Honey," she said, her voice weak, "I've been in an accident. I've been hurt."

I sighed, "I don't have time for silly jokes at the moment. Come on."

There were noises and other people's voices in the background, then Jon spoke into the phone, "André, It's Jon. Listen, Charlie was burned—it's really bad. You need to get here now."

"What are you talking about?" I asked, my heart rate picking up.

"I just sent you a photo."

As my phone lit up, I could hardly believe what I was seeing. The image was of Charlie's body, completely seared—discolored, angry and red, "Oh my God!" I yelled, "I'll be right there!"

"Get here as soon as you can," Jon replied.

My voice cracked as I yelled out to my mom, "Charlie was in an accident, take care of the boys!"

I grabbed my wallet and my house keys, then ran out into the driveway and suddenly remembered the keys to my car; they were with Charlie. I paced in the driveway for a moment, cursing my useless car before looking to the left and noticing there were no cars in our neighbors' driveway—they were out for the day. I then looked over to the neighbor's house on my right. There were two cars in their driveway, so I took off toward their house. I ran across the driveway and onto the grass, stumbling on the spaces between the hard and soft surfaces. My feet sank on the grass and pounded on the pavement as I landed on his walkway and bolted up the staircase. Once there, I banged on the door, trying to catch my breath while I waited for our neighbor, Kirk, to get to the door.

He opened it without urgency and said, "Hey man, what's going on?"

"Charlie's been in an accident," I yelled, startling him. "She has my keys. Can I borrow your car to get to her?"

"Of course, of course. Go!" He fumbled in his pocket for the keys and tossed them to me.

I ran to the car, flung the door open and got in. The unfamiliar smell of the car hit me as I searched for the button to start the car, then remembered I needed to shove the key into the ignition and turn it. As the car rumbled to life, I placed my hand on the passenger's headrest, turned my head, and backed out of the driveway, peeling out with a screech. Thoughts bolted and flashed through my mind like lightning on a summer night, streaking the darkness with light. Images of the argument the night before mingled with those about what would greet me when I got to Charlie's side. I wished I'd pushed harder—forced her to stay home—prevented this whole mess.

My body jostled with each bump as I careened onto the highway toward the brewery. Compared to my SUV, Kurt's sedan felt like a go-cart—tiny and close to the ground. The sun shone through the driver's side window casting a hot, pulsing glow on my left arm and the side of my face. I pushed my foot onto the gas so hard the pedal nearly touched the floorboard. I reached out and fiddled with the air conditioner's knob, trying to get it to blow cool air but I was trapped by the heat, held hostage by the moment. I rolled down the window in desperation, the smell of exhaust stinging my nostrils. I wanted to scream Charlie's name, to look over and see her next to me, to wake up from this nightmare. Yet the roar of the air and the rumble of the asphalt beneath the small car kept me locked into the road ahead. I imagined what would happen if a cop pulled up behind me, lights flashing, siren wailing. I knew exactly what I'd do.

I'd keep racing.

Just as I merged onto I-64 headed toward the brewery, my phone rang. I struggled to grab it as I kept my eyes on the road.

"Hello?" I called.

"Hello, is this Charlie's husband?"

"Yes! I'm on my way!"

"This is a nurse who was just with Charlie—they're airlifting her to UVA hospital. You should get there as soon as you can."

I drew a sharp breath as I realized I was heading in the opposite direction. "I'm turning around now," I said, then hung up the phone and asked Siri to get me directions to UVA. I tossed the phone onto the passenger seat and rolled up the window just as Siri directed me get off the highway and turn around.

My eyes scanned the sky, searching for the helicopter with my wife in it. Yet, the sky was blank; an empty expanse of blue flecked with small clouds, reminding me of the sawdust in Charlie's hair.

My phone rang again.

"Hello?" I yelled into the phone.

"Hello André? It's me again, listen, Charlie is actually being taken to Virginia Commonwealth University Medical Center (VCU). I'm sorry to make you turn around, but. . ."

"It's fine," I said then hung up and tossed my phone aside before turning the car around once more, yelling to Siri for updated directions.

I looked down at the dash expecting to see the familiar count of miles the car's gasoline would take me; instead, there was a gauge that hovered right above the halfway mark. I clenched my teeth and gripped the wheel, praying there was enough gas in the car to get me to Charlie. I wove in and out of traffic, the car responding violently to every move I made. I imagined the car flipping, the glass exploding around me, the metal wrapping around my body, leaving me even more helpless than I was now. I batted the thought from my mind and stomped on the gas.

Forty-five minutes later, I flung the car into a parking spot at VCU, grabbed the keys and my wallet and bounded out of the car door. My body cut through the summer heat as I ran toward the doors, which slid open to reveal chaos. My eyes, used to the sting of the sun, squinted as I pulled on my mask and raced to the metal detector. Kids were screaming, people were yelling, and I was tossing my personal effects into a bowl the same way I did at the airport. The security guard nodded and I grabbed my things and raced toward the front desk where a young blond nurse sat calmly tapping on her keyboard.

"Hi," I said as my body hit the edge of the desk, "My name is André Xavier. My wife is being brought here by helicopter. Her name is Charlie Xavier."

"Okay, sir. Just give me a minute please."

Once again, she tapped on her computer, adjusting her mask as she leaned closer to her screen, looking for Charlie's name. My fingers drummed the desk as a woman in scrubs came up to the nurse, leaned down, and said, "This is Trauma Dublin."

The nurse kept a straight face as she nodded, then looked up at me and said, "Okay, Mr. Xavier, we've been waiting for you."

"What does Trauma Dublin mean? I'm here for Charlie. . ."

The nurse at the computer responded, "We use trauma names because they instantly alert staff that their care needs to be expedited. Charlie is Trauma Dublin."

The nurse who'd whispered to her came around the desk and said, "Can you please come with me?"

I followed her down the hallway, our shoes squeaking on the sterile tile floor. We walked through a large, clunking set of doors where the hallway gave way to a larger area with a bank of elevators to the left and a Panera Bread straight ahead. To the right was a room with a handwritten sign on it that read "emergency waiting area."

The nurse ushered me through the doors and told me to wait there and that the phone in the room would ring when they had news for me.

The room was lined with chairs. It was silent except for a large television murmuring in the corner. I was alone except for an older man staring blankly at the TV and a younger man on his phone who sat on opposite sides of the room, each trapped in their own version of a nightmare. I sat down and pulled out my phone to try and tap out a text to Charlie's family to let them know what had happened. Yet, I didn't know what to say or how to say it because I had no information. I knew her injuries must be bad, but it never occurred to me that they could be fatal. Though concerned and plagued with anxiety, I wasn't scared.

I just wanted to see my wife.

Minutes ticked by, gathering in the ether until they became more than an hour. My throat stung with thirst. I stood up and walked out of the room, noticing a vending machine that sold water. I fed it two dollars and a bottle of water rumbled through the machine and tumbled out to me. I cracked the seal, pulled down my mask, and guzzled.

Back in the waiting room, I was now alone. Both men had long since been called away, leaving me with only my thoughts. I looked at the phone, which hadn't rung, so I decided to pick it up and press "0" in hopes I would connect with someone who could help me.

The phone crackled to life, "How can I help you?"

"Hello," I said, my voice wobbling. "This is André Xavier, I've been waiting for more than an hour for someone to call about my wife, Charlie. Is there anyone coming to give me information?"

I heard the clicking of computer keys then the voice said, "Yes, Mr. Xavier. Someone is on the way to talk to you now. I'm sorry for the delay."

"It's fine," I said, then hung up the phone.

I walked back to the chair that was now familiar to me—it still held some of my body's warmth.

Another 30 minutes ticked by before a female voice softly called out, "Mr. Xavier?"

I looked up from my phone to see a young chaplain with dark, straight hair standing in the doorway.

"Yes?" I replied.

The chaplain approached me and sat next to me. "I'm Lizzie," she said, reaching out her hand to shake mine. "Tell me about your wife."

"Well, Charlie is a great wife and an amazing person, she's a wonderful mom to our two boys. She's been working so hard lately on yet another business we're opening together, I just wish I knew what happened and ..."

"I know you're anxious to see her."

I nodded.

"Okay, Mr. Xavier, we're going to head up to the burn unit now. Just follow me," she said as she stood, smoothing her black pants.

I followed her down the hallway toward the elevators. Together, we waited, then stepped into the one whose doors slid open. We rode in silence until we reached the eighth floor. As soon as I stepped through the elevator doors, the energy changed. Tears slid down my face as I took in the sights and smells—the pieces of equipment against the walls, the sterile smell of bandages and hand sanitizer. The thought that Charlie was somewhere in that place caused my throat to close and my stomach to flip.

The chaplain led me to another waiting area where was sat together. In that cold chair, emotions flooded out of me. The chaplain reached over, took my hand, came close to me and said, "Let's say a prayer together."

As I closed my eyes, a gush of hot tears cascaded down my face. I listened to her words intently, trying to feel the prayer, allowing God to envelop me in His infinite comfort, but no comfort came. I couldn't pray this feeling away.

It wasn't long before Charlie's doctor entered the room with a nurse. He wore scrubs and a cap—the kind surgeons wear when they are working on a patient. With them was a man I came to know as our case manager.

"Mr. Xavier, I'm Doctor Bergin. Let's head to another room to chat."

I stood and walked with the entourage down the hallway. The feeling of being with a group of people who knew what was going on with Charlie while I was still in the dark was eerie—like I was about to be let in on a secret I was desperate to know but wasn't sure I was ready to hear.

A heavy set of doors opened, and we headed down another cavernous hallway in the maze of the hospital. Straight ahead was the burn unit waiting area with a kids' waiting area across the hall. We made a left through the first one, which led to a conference room. I took a seat on a couch in front of a large window, which overlooked the sun-drenched parking lot where people scurried to and from their cars. The chaplain sat next to me, and Dr. Bergin pulled up a chair directly across from me, flanked by the nurse and case worker on each side.

"Mr. Xavier," Dr. Bergin began, "What can you tell me about Charlie?"

"Well, we'll be married for 13 years in just a few weeks. We have two kids and. . ."

"Two kids?" he interrupted. "How old are they?"

"They are two boys, four-years and ten-months-old," I replied.

Without words, he took his hat off and held his head in his hands.

I looked at the chaplain as if to ask, "What's going on?"

She looked back at me with her brows knitted together; she slid closer to me.

I tried to get a question out to Dr. Bergin, but nothing came.

He looked up at me with tears flooding his piercing, ice blue eyes.

"Doctor," I finally managed, "Is my wife alive?"

After a few, torturous moments he replied, "She is, but she was very, very badly injured. She suffered incredibly deep wounds."

My stomach lurched. My palms were wet as I imagined the looks on our sons' faces as I told them what happened to mommy. I drew a breath and asked, "What are her chances?"

"Excuse me?" Dr. Bergin replied.

"What are her chances of survival?" I asked.

He paused, then said in a solemn tone, "I would say less than 30 percent."

"Oh God," I whispered as I sat back in the chair. "Oh God, oh God."

The chaplain squeezed my hand.

"But I promise you this," Dr. Bergin said, "We will not torture your wife. If at any given moment, I feel like she's not responding to the treatment, we will not continue."

I could barely breathe. Charlie could be ripped from me.

After all, they said they'd try, but if nothing seemed to be working, no heroic efforts would be made.

Instead, they'd just give up.

CHAPTER 2

Before

I'm originally from Brazil and when I was in my early twenties I was on an 18-month work visa, training in hotel management at the Clifton Inn in Charlottesville, Virginia. I'd spend my days learning the ins and outs of everything from guest experience to handling complaints and crises. It was an experience I planned to take with me to my regular job on a luxury cruise line. After work, exhausted and ready to relax, I would return to my apartment. Every time I stepped foot on the property, I prayed that I would see the leasing manager. Charlie.

With her golden blond hair, sweet, sometimes devilish smile, and her deep blue eyes, I was immediately drawn to her. I wish I could say something romantic like I looked at her and felt our souls mingle or that anytime I came into contact with her, I just knew she was *the one*. Truthfully, I just thought she was beautiful and would have given anything for just one date with her. But she was so stunning, so outgoing, so vivacious, and smart that I knew she was so far out of my league that the chances of her saying yes were next to nothing.

But I wouldn't stop hoping.

Anytime I walked into the office to pay rent or to ask a question, I'd try to work up the courage to ask her out, though all that typically came out was a quick, "Hi, how are you?" or a casual nod in her direction. I wished I had a reason to talk to her—some excuse to sit down and chat with her at length, but I had nothing, and I just couldn't force myself to walk up to her and say something without some way to break the ice. Thankfully, God always intervenes in matters of fate.

A few of my friends from Brazil were coming to train at the local IHOP restaurant and had decided to rent an apartment at the same property where I was living. I was their guarantor for the lease, so I had to go to Charlie's office to do the paperwork.

I will never forget that feeling; the butterflies, the sweaty palms, the attempts to act cool despite my roaring nerves. After the papers were signed and my friends' leases were ready to go, I stood, but I couldn't make myself move. My heart was directing my every move. Hands in my pockets, eyes looking into hers, I managed, "Would you like to go to dinner sometime?"

She smiled.

My stomach flipped.

Her eyebrows flickered.

Then she said it. . .

No, I'm sorry.

My stomach dropped.

She explained that it wouldn't be appropriate for her to go on a date with a resident of the property and I understood, although I was disappointed. Yet, as I turned to leave, leasing paperwork in hand, something inside me told me not to give up.

Two weeks later, I asked her out again.

She said no.

One week after that, I asked her out again.

She said no.

I did this every week until I could see I was starting to wear her down. Finally, the perfect opportunity arose, I said "Listen, my friends are having a party tonight. Why don't you meet me there and we can hang out?"

Then she asked with an eyebrow raised, "As friends?"

I stood still and calmly smiled back, though my insides were celebrating, jumping up and down, punching the air. "Great," I said. I'll see you tonight."

That night was a swirl of significant exchanges that left me wanting more. We had so many similarities and were so compatible in so many ways, our connection was quick, and conversation flowed easily—a tangle of *me too*'s and *I agree*'s. Even though Charlie was only 20 and I was 23, we shared a maturity well beyond our years. It turned out, Charlie had moved out of her parent's home when she was 17 and lived on her own, giving her a sense of pragmatism and instincts that were sharp and steady. I had worked for many years on a cruise ship providing management services, so I had the wisdom that extensive traveling affords. We were both go-getters with jobs in industries we enjoyed, and neither of us was willing to settle for anything other than our personal best. We spent the entire evening talking, tucked away in a corner as her friends surrounded us, drinking in all that is life in our early twenties.

Following that evening, Charlie, who had once seemed so out of my league became *my person*. We were inseparable, spending as much time as we possibly could together. Those early days were filled with stolen kisses, significant conversation, and sweet exchanges—all of which added up to a special kind of love—our love.

Charlie and I found ourselves in a difficult position. We had just 11 months until I would lose my work visa and would return to my work on the cruise line. But Charlie and I were so entangled, braided together in ways only love provides, we decided I couldn't leave. Instead, we decided to get married. With my Visa expiration looming, just a few months later in January, we decided to have a quick wedding at the courthouse. There were no huge bouquets of flowers, no long lists of guests, or extravagant things. There was just Charlie, me, and her parents as Charlie and I joined hands and said our vows.

As satisfactory as that wedding was, Charlie and I wanted the big celebration with all of our friends and family. Less than a year later, in October, we had a big wedding at a luxe winery not far from our home.

That day—our *real* wedding day—was one of the greatest days of my life.

Charlie standing at the end of the aisle, radiant and beaming.

Reaching her and holding her hands tight, staring into her twinkling eyes.

Honoring Christ.

Making promises.

Exchanging rings.

Indulging the madness in our love.

As the years ticked by, Charlie and I worked hard, and I mean *hard*. Charlie kept her job at the apartment complex, then eventually moved into marketing. Following my training, I spent some building my dream career at the Clifton Inn Hotel before moving to another luxury resort, Keswick Hall and finally the Four Seasons D.C., and one day I realized that I would never achieve real wealth and time freedom until I started my own company—a travel agency that allowed me to leverage my experience in hotel management and my extensive world travels. As my businesses expanded and we began to experienced success, we purchased our first home that was just right for us. We lived life so intensely, we traveled extensively, our love for each other kept growing day by day, we took our time developing a strong foundation to our marriage before having kids. We were growing alongside one another and were becoming a power couple to be reckoned with.

Charlie and I had decided to wait about five years before we started trying to get pregnant and we really enjoyed those years by traveling and letting our love and respect for one another flourish. By year eight, we still weren't pregnant, so at the suggestion of our doctor, we decided to try in vitro fertilization (IVF). This came with rounds and rounds of shots for Charlie, her hormones all over the place, her body exhausted. Anytime she became frustrated or felt sick, we tried to remain conscious of what was to come: our first baby.

The day of the embryo transfer felt like it was years in the making—because it was. Charlie and I went to the doctors' office feeling giddy, as if we were to have the baby that very day. Charlie put on a hospital gown, prepared herself, and the procedure began. Her hand in mine, Charlie and I watched as the doctor implanted the egg that we believed would be our first child. I'll never forget the look she gave me, eyes filled to the brim with tears, when the procedure was over and the embryo was finally nestled in her womb.

Later that day, Charlie was relaxed in bed when her phone rang. Charlie's dad had been battling cancer for 20 years, since she was just a young girl. She received news that her father's cancer was back and had moved to his spinal cord. The doctors told him he might have five or six months to live, which devastated Charlie as she and her dad were extremely close. We gathered our things and rushed to her parent's house to lend our support and spend some time with her father after the startling news. To our complete shock, Charlie's father passed away that very night. Not long after, we found out that the embryo transfer hadn't taken.

Charlie was in pure anguish.

Not surprisingly, it took us a year to begin to talk about having children again. We both hated to think about fertility treatments. After our experience, we knew the disappointment of not getting pregnant and assumed experiencing that stress month after month could really wear on Charlie's well-being. Since Charlie had converted to Catholicism one year earlier, we decided to talk to the priest about adopting. Yet as we sat in our seats across the desk from the priest, we had no idea just how unnecessary the conversation would be.

Charlie was already pregnant.

Our elation over our pregnancy was almost too intense to describe. We were so thrilled, in fact, that we couldn't wait to find out the gender of our baby. We went to a third party, novelty service provider who placed a slip of paper with the gender on it into a sealed envelope, which we then handed to a dear friend who planned a gender reveal party.

On the day of the party, forty friends and family members gathered. As they arrived, we handed out canisters. In unison, guests shouted "1, 2, 3," and we shot off the cannons, launching pink powder, confetti, and glitter cascading into the air. Everyone jumped for joy, exclaiming just how lucky we were. We were lucky alright—just lucky in a different way than we thought.

Just days after the gender reveal party at Charlie's first ultrasound, the tech asked, "Do you want to know the sex of the baby?"

Just days after the gender reveal party at Charlie's first ultrasound, the tech asked, "Do you want to know the sex of the baby?"

Charlie beamed, "Oh no, it's okay. We already know it's a girl!"

The tech smiled wide and responded, "Well, if it's a girl, then she has an extra leg!"

Charlie and I laughed, grasping one another's hands, taking in the shock and humor of it all. We were on our way to welcoming wild boy—London—to the family!

The whole pregnancy with London brought us so much happiness and joy. There were cravings and cradle building, nursery decoration, family celebrations, and all the wonderful things that come with expectant parenthood.

London's birth went smoothly and just two days later, we were discharged from the hospital. We were so grateful to be home, living with London in the spaces we'd set up just for him. For hours on end, Charlie and I would stare at him, in awe of the splendor of this tiny body.

Then, just one week after London was born, Charlie's grandmother sadly passed away, so we packed up our little family and made the drive to Bristol, Virginia for the funeral. We arrived at the hotel and Charlie wasn't feeling well. She had a high fever and was sweating profusely. We called Charlie's labor and delivery nurse and from what Charlie described she said it seemed like it could be mastitis. She suggested that we get Charlie checked out at the local emergency room since she needed special care—Charlie had Rheumatoid Arthritis and therefore had special needs as a patient.

The hospital was packed and we ended up sitting on a stretcher in the hallway with our newborn for hours that night. The first doctor diagnosed the mastitis and prescribed antibiotics. Thank goodness the second doctor noticed Charlie had RA and asked if he could run more tests. It turned out, Charlie was septic. They finally transferred us to the maternity ward and Charlie stayed there for 7 grueling days. On day 5, Charlie had still not reacted to any of the antibiotics they were giving her. Her breasts were still red and inflamed and she was in agony.

I will never forget the doctor who came in to deliver some news, "I don't know if you have family, but I am warning you that you may have to make arrangements."

My wife is going to die.

I was terrified, but I wasn't going to accept this as our truth, so I called a local priest who rushed to Charlie's bedside. There in the maternity ward where life is the dominant force, we were battling death. Charlie received a sacrament called The Anointing of the Sick, which helps bring Jesus' healing power to those who are seriously injured or ill. The prayer was miraculous, the antibiotics that were not working, started to work with two days after the priest blessing.

Things started to improve.

The swelling went down.

The sepsis was cured.

Life came back into Charlie's eyes.

That was when I first learned the truth about my wife: she is a fighter, a maven of miracles, a superhero.

Three years later, we found ourselves pregnant again, this time with another boy we'd name Julien. During Charlie's pregnancy with Julien, the COVID-19 pandemic hit. Prior to that, our businesses had been wildly successful and our lives looked exactly like we always dreamed they would. We had built considerable business success; at that time, we owned or part owned four different businesses and we were planning to start a fifth: a travel agency, a tour operating business, a wedding and events transportation company, a hop-on tour business, and had just purchased an old VFW hall where we would start Patch brewery. Charlie was a stay-at-home mom and my business partner, an active participant in many community mom's clubs, doing everything she was put here on this Earth to do. I was doing the same, and man, was I proud. Having arrived in the United States and landing a starting position, I'd gone from making $10 an hour to running our businesses and doing what I was innately good at.

But this plague threatened it all.

Every industry was being hit hard by the COVID-19 pandemic, but the hospitality industry—which all of our businesses were tied into—was hit harder than most. In the span of a month, all five of our businesses shut down. Every day I would watch the news, staring at the scrolling statistics about death rates, the stock market, and letting global anxiety envelop me. At that time, 100 percent of our financial stability was tied into my career, not to mention 98 percent of my current identity. My work gave me recognition and status and was, therefore, most responsible for my confidence and self-worth. This means the threat of a loss of any kind tied to work is tied directly back to my sense of self-worth. Day after day, as Charlie's belly grew, so did my resolve. I just wanted to assign some kind of *meaning* and purpose to something that seemed so incomprehensible.

"I have all this time on my hands now," I said to Charlie as she rested her hands on her belly, "I'm going to use it wisely. I'm going to find ways to improve as a businessman so I can find a way around this mess."

I went onto my iPad and began to download as many highly-recommended business books as I could find. I devoured them all. I started with self-help author, Napoleon Hill. Then, I read all of Tony Robbins' books. I was looking to soak up all the knowledge about business and leadership-development that I could. I completely ignored anything that would help me develop personally—in my mind, I didn't need that. It wasn't practical. Before this time, I had always touted that I wanted more time with my family and I did dream of that, but as my businesses grew, and my confidence expanded at the same rate, I became more and more obsessed with the growth of my business instead of my heart and my mind. I was comfortable with my hardening heart, especially when it meant my business would not only be back on track, it would skyrocket at a time when others were experiencing failure.

When Julien arrived, we were one of the many couples forced to navigate giving birth during the pandemic.

Masks on faces.

Hands holding hands.

Deep, purposeful breaths.

Beads of sweat.

A baby's cry.

Our family had grown by one.

By the time Julien was five or six months old, my mom had not even met him. With the near-global lockdown breathing down our necks and the uncertainness of what acquiring COVID-19 could do to our health, I found it imperative for mom to meet Julien. We couldn't go to Brazil. There was a travel ban in place. So, we planned for Charlie and the boys to meet my mom in Mexico where there wasn't a travel ban in place while I stayed home and worked. We'd allow my mom to quarantine there while she visited with Charlie and the kids. After a week in Mexico, Charlie would bring London back home, and I would fly out to spend another week with my mom and Julien, then my mom would fly back to the U.S. with Julien and me. It was a perfect plan.

When we got back to Virginia, mom wasn't feeling well, so we tested her for COVID-19 and it was negative. The next day, I heard a thump upstairs, and when I ran into her room, she was on the floor next to the bed.

"What happened?" I asked frantically.

"I don't know. I guess I passed out," she responded, her voice weak.

We took her immediately to the E.R. where she tested positive for COVID-19. She stayed in the hospital for five days, fighting it off.

Of course, after that, the whole house tested positive for COVID-19 before it was over with. Charlie's doctor told her to go off her arthritis medications while her system battled COVID-19 since her meds suppress the immune system.

Thank goodness that happened the way it did because, at the time of Charlie's accident, she was off her immunosuppressants, which gave her a leg up on the healing process after the explosion.

Now, sitting with the chaplain staring down the hallway at the hospital, all I could think about was Charlie, the ways I loved her and the ways I wish I'd loved her, and all the ways I'd taken her for granted. As I was led down the hallway, the doctor's words rang in my ears:

We will not torture your wife.

CHAPTER 3

After

Before we made the final trek to Charlie's room, I was led into a small triage area to get suited up. I was fitted with a blue plastic apron, gloves, and my regular fabric mask was replaced with a more robust N-95. Due to general mask mandates and precautionary measures, I was well acquainted with wearing a mask, but the rest of the protective gear was new to me. My hands felt hot inside the gloves as I struggled to get the apron to lie flat. I took in the sterile smell of the room. I could hardly believe this was my reality. Just the day before, instead of arguing with Charlie, I could have reached out and rubbed her neck for her. I could have encouraged her. I could have hugged her. Now, a door was being opened for me and I was being led down what seemed like a mile-long hallway past glass boxes, each displaying a victim of hungry flames.

Finally, we arrived at Charlie's room and I peered through the glass. There, my wife, the mother of my children, lay on a bed, wrapped up in white bandages like a mummy in a sterile sarcophagus, with a tube coming out of her mouth. The IV tower next to her must have had 20 different lines hooked to it and so many bags, each one fought for space. Leave it to Charlie to muster a partial smile and wave her burned, mitten-covered hands to signal to me that she was alright. That's Charlie—always thinking about someone else.

Slowly, I entered the glass box, which I soon learned was a negative pressure room—a room that has its own filtering system so the air inside doesn't circulate through the rest of the hospital. I walked over to the bed and stood next to her, my heart racing. That was the moment I saw my wife's face for the first time since the accident. I looked down at her, trying to process what I was seeing. Her face was five times its normal size, causing her features to look stretched and distorted. The whites of her eyes bulged so intensely that they looked like Jell-O.

I leaned in and whispered, "Charlie, honey, I love you so much."

I choked back tears.

Intubated and unable to talk, Charlie motioned that she wanted a piece of paper and something to write with. I turned to the nurse, who scrambled for a pen and a clipboard. I placed the pen in Charlie's bandaged hand and held out the clipboard for her. She wrote:

I am fucking tired of not knowing the time!
Please take my lunchbox out of the car. It has a tuna sandwich in it.
Buy baby food for Julien. We are out!

I couldn't help but smile … just a little. Charlie—my Charlie—was still in there, and that meant only one thing. Percentages and likelihood of survival didn't matter.

She was going to fight.

CHAPTER 4

72-Hours

Staring at Charlie's wishes in black and white broke the tension in the room, bringing a little levity to the situation. Although I was able to smile at her words, the raw humanity of Charlie's request nearly broke me. She could have scribbled anything, yet, practical and loving as ever, she thought of her sons, a smelly mess in the car, and her base desire to know the time.

Right away, I had the nurse move the clock from the wall behind her to the wall in front of her so she could see the time and I promised I would handle her lunch box and the baby's food. She then asked me for her glasses and her phone charger, which I promised to bring. Then, I pulled out my phone and showed her pictures of our family. Though her face was huge, skin taut, her smile was unmistakable as she stared at the photos of our boys. I closed my eyes.

First date.

Glistening blond hair.

Those eyes.

That smile.

Looking her over once more, I couldn't comprehend what had happened and how. Via text and calls in the waiting room, I was able to patch together a rough idea of the events that led to us being here. Charlie was almost finished sanding a wood frame to a black board for the kids, using an electric sander. There was a gasoline container on the floor near her. Charlie slipped on what we believe to be gas on the floor. She fell and her hand holding the sander touched the concrete floor, causing a spark followed by an immediate explosion. Charlie was engulfed in a flame ball. She managed to crawl out of the flames, stood up and took six steps while she was on fire, getting outside of the pavilion structure and dropping and rolling until she was no longer on fire. She then stood up and took a seat at a picnic table; her body completely charred..

A nurse—and the wife of the fire chief—happened to be in the parking lot after shopping at a grocery store right next to Patch. She heard about the emergency and was on the scene within three minutes. She quickly assessed the severity of Charlie's injuries. She told Jon, who by then was on the phone with 911 that Charlie needed a helicopter ASAP. That was all I knew, but at that moment, what happened didn't really matter.

All that mattered was Charlie.

As I scanned Charlie's body in the bed, all I could see were bandages, tubes, wires, and whirring machines. I did not understand the extent, nor could I even comprehend the severity of her injuries. In those first few moments, all I was focused on was Charlie, her needs, and how I could possibly meet them. My focus wouldn't stay that narrow for long.

As time crawled by, I lived on water alone. I could not eat; I didn't feel hungry, I barely slept. All I felt was pain. The doctors kept reinforcing the fact that this first leg of the race was going to be a full-on rollercoaster and they continued to remind me just how serious Charlie situation was. Over and over and over again, doctors reminded me that the first 72-hours were crucial. Once a body is burned as extensively as Charlie's—and some parts were burned down to the bone—all it knows to do is protect itself, so the body starts to pull all of its own fluids, blood included, to the main vital organs. Despite the body's efforts, many times, the redirecting of these fluids leads to death. To avoid this happening, doctors pump a ton of fluids into the body to keep it alive, which puts the system into a hypermetabolic state. That means the body's system switches from running at 100 percent capacity to running at 300 percent capacity, a level at which many bodies simply cannot handle. The heart just can't keep up with the body's demand to heal.

While navigating the first 24 of those 72 hours, I lived like a zombie, only going back and forth between the hospital and home, working my entire schedule for the week around visiting hours. With every minute that passed, things became even more overwhelming and I began to feel like I was drowning. I had 30 or 40 messages on my phone from loved ones, friends, and acquaintances checking on Charlie, and even though I couldn't return all of them, one of them happened to be a good friend who had lost a daughter to a rare genetic disease three years prior. I decided to answer his call since I knew he'd have a basic understanding of what I was going through as we fought for Charlie's life. As I lamented about worrying about my ability to keep up with caring for Charlie, the kids, and keeping everyone updated he said, "When we went through our struggle with our daughter, I felt overwhelmed with all the requests for updates too. You know what I did? I started to journal updates to send out to everyone. It really helped me and it might help you too. I'm praying for you guys.

As we hung up the call, I stared straight ahead trying to imagine myself writing a public journal for all to see. I knew I made grammatical mistakes and Charlie always gave me a hard time for it, but I decided I'd rather deal with the stress of unanswered messages than the stress of trying to write English in any way that made sense. I pushed the idea out of my head and went on with my day, wishing the first 72-hours would just come to an end so Charlie could get on with fighting the big fight.

That first evening, In the dark of night, I lay splayed across the bed, my arms clenching pillows, hands grazing Charlie's empty side of the bed as I sobbed. Although I knew Charlie well enough to know that she was a worthy adversary, even with the odds stacked against her, I couldn't get that figure out of my mind.

Less than 30 percent.

On the second day, I walked into the hospital to find Charlie was restrained with cloth handcuffs. I rushed to her side, wondering what I should do next. Should I call the nurse to untie her ... free her myself ... try to get a doctor's attention? Noticing my distress, Charlie's nurse came over and placed her hand on my shoulder.

"I know, it's a shock," she said, her voice soft and kind. "We tried to induce a coma to aid in the healing process, but Charlie is strong and is fighting off the meds, so it didn't take. She's been trying to pull out her ventilator tube, so this is the only option available to us."

I shook her hand off my shoulder and leaned over, my mouth near Charlie's ear. I whispered, "Keep doing what you're doing. You need to keep fighting."

She nodded her head then began to move her lips. If I leaned close enough, I could understand some of the things she tried to say to me.

"How are the boys?" she mouthed.

Of course, that was at the top of Charlie's list of need-to-knows. I pulled out my phone and showed her pictures of both of them from that morning with sleepy eyes and tousled hair. I told her all about the evening before and that morning, what the kids ate, what they played, and how much they missed Mommy.

Not long after, Charlie began to tire. Her arms went slack, held up by the cloth handcuffs in an odd position as she slept. I pulled my chair as close to Charlie as I could, feeling claustrophobic in my dressing gown, gloves, and mask. Her room was kept at 85 degrees at all times, I wanted to shed them like a snake sheds his skin, to unravel Charlie's bandages and to find this was all a misunderstanding. I wanted to hold her, to run, to go back to *before*.

Yet, there we were, stuck in a now that I would do anything to escape.

As Charlie slept, I let my mind wander. I thought about the days and weeks before the accident, the way we lived our lives, our deep love, my hard heart. I was finally in a place where I wasn't sobbing, I wasn't wishing or praying, I was sitting in the feelings that had settled inside me. In that moment, I was finally able to name what I was feeling: *Fear*.

Before the accident, Charlie and I could look into the future and see a clear picture of what it would look like. We knew our businesses would continue to grow, as would our sons. We'd work together to build an empire, eventually able to embrace our financial freedom and travel. Now, nothing was sure, nor was it even remotely predictable. It was impossible for me to picture what our future could possibly look like. I tried, but nothing came. Instead of that hope I once had, fear filled me like the fluids pumped into Charlie's swollen body.

Several hours later, Dr. Bergin came to see us. Puffy-eyed and exhausted, I watched as he looked over Charlie, checking her vitals and going over information with the nurse. It was then he finally introduced me to any kind of a timeline that went past the retched first 72-hours.

Together, we stepped into the hallway and he said, "I think it's time we begin talking about what healing will look like as we move through the most critical stage. However, make no mistake, things will remain critical for a long, long time."

I nodded.

"Based on my last patient with burns as severe as Charlie's, we can expect her to be in the hospital for a year or more. Recoveries of this kind are a rollercoaster. . ."

I sighed. I'd heard that analogy a thousand times.

"The good news is," he continued, "Charlie's organs haven't failed. As a matter of fact, in the first 48 hours after a burn like this, most people's kidneys fail and they need dialysis because there is just too much fluid going through the body for the kidneys to process. Most people's bodies just give up."

Clearly, Dr. Bergin didn't know Charlie.

But he would.

On day three, I found myself holding my breath nearly all day. This was it, the day that would take us to the 72-hour mark—our first milestone. Up until that day, I was still living on water and bread, had little to no sleep, and found myself hungry for only one thing—Charlie's safe recovery. The seconds crawled by as I prayed we'd move from moment to moment without incident, which we did.

Charlie's demands on that day were for me to send pictures and videos of the boys to her phone so she had updated things to watch. She also wanted me to tell the nurses to be gentle when moving her legs. Though she rarely complained, the symptoms of her arthritis made her legs stiff and swollen; symptoms made far worse by the extra fluid in her body. It was painful to bend her legs and she wanted to make sure the nurses knew that to avoid further discomfort.

The last thing she asked was for me to kiss her on the forehead. I was already a step ahead of her on that one. My lips found their way to the spot above her brows just as the clock struck hour 72.

That Sunday, Dr. Bergin came in to talk to Charlie and me about her upcoming skin grafting procedures—and there were slated to be many. Dr. Bergin explained that 85 percent of her skin was burned off of Charlie's body, and she needed a makeshift covering quickly to guard against infection, inflammation, and all sorts of other possibly-fatal contaminations. The first mission was debridement, or removal, of the remaining dead tissue. Meanwhile, the doctors would send off a sample of Charlie's good skin to a lab so they could test it and see if they'd be able to grow new skin to replace the nonviable tissue. Dr. Bergin told us that they were going to start that process the very next day. He went on to explain that he really wanted me to be prepared because things were going to get rough.

CEA (Culture Epidermal Autograft) are wound covering grafts composed of the patient's own skin cells. Since Charlie didn't have enough skin to donate for an autograft, the doctors had to use a procedure where they harvest her own skin cells to grow more of them in a lab. The problem with CEA skin is that it is not natural. It is frail and easily damaged. The doctors tell us there will be many years of physiotherapy to keep the scar tissue that is going to build up from limiting Charlie's movement. She will also be dealing with joint damage from her arthritis that will go untreated during this upcoming period.

As Dr. Bergin left the room, I could see Charlie moving her lips. I leaned in close, stared at her lips, and deciphered her saying, "How am I doing?"

I told her, "Charlie, you are doing amazing. You are responding so well. Your body is so strong. I am so proud of you."

Finally, on Monday morning, I ate breakfast. Actually, mom forced me to eat breakfast. I had French bread with butter and cheese and a cup of coffee with milk.

Satiated, I packed up my things and headed to the hospital, which had become my routine. I was no longer focused on our businesses at all. I was laser-focused on Charlie. It felt like my life had stopped on the day of the accident.

When I got to the hospital, once I was suited up, the first person I saw was Dr. Bergin, who seemed almost upbeat. "André, I have good news. I sent a skin sample to the lab early this morning. It looks like they'll be able to grow her skin. This is a really big deal."

"Amazing!" I replied. "Tell me more about the procedure and how the growth of skin works."

Dr. Bergin was uncharacteristically animated, which I took as an excellent sign. As he spoke, I imagined a printer churning out sheets of Charlie's skin that they'd be able to stitch on with minimal effort. They'd piece my wife back together and we'd be home before I knew it. Then I heard him utter the phrase "Twelve weeks." It would take twelve weeks for her skin to grow in the lab.

Nothing medical is simple.

After that, little nuggets of information about our uphill climb kept flowing in. Later that day, Dr. Bergin introduced me to Dr. Roland, who was the Director of the ICU team. He was in charge of everything but performing the surgeries. He was a kind man from Bolivia and we talked about our countries of origin for a while. Then, he got straight to it. "I am telling you right now, infection is the one thing you have to be worried about. When a patient comes into the ICU, they start at a five percent chance of infection. The chance of infection grows exponentially over time—meaning the patient is at a 100 percent chance of infection after 30 days. Statistically, I can almost guarantee you that she will have a major infection every 30 days she is here. And yes, they can be fatal, but we are able to treat *most* of them."

Most?

"...every time I go to see her, I come out stronger. She is an amazing inspiration. I have to ask you to keep praying and sending positive vibes; it is working. She is really fighting hard, and doctors and nurses are beyond amazed with her progress so far."

—Excerpt From Journal Entry September 11, 2021

CHAPTER 5

Journal

By the end of week one, voicemail messages were piling up. The first 30 or 40 messages quickly turned into 50 or 60. Every time I looked at my phone, my stomach flipped and my heart fell. There was no possible way I could get back to everyone. I thought about what my friend told me about writing updates I could send out to everyone at once.

Charlie's mom's friends had already created an initial Facebook page that was the hub for close friends. As I sat in the hospital watching Charlie sleep, I gazed at my phone and decided to type out a message that I could post on the page. I began typing, "Good Evening, Friends. I just want to start by saying THANK YOU! Your love and support is nothing short of amazing! Thank you from the bottom of my heart." From there, I typed a short update about Charlie, her current condition, and what we could expect next.

I navigated to the page, opened the window, copied and pasted the text and hit "post." Just as I did, a wave of relief washed over me. Not only had I updated everyone all at once, but I had given *myself* time to write and reflect on what had been going on. Even if it was just a few minutes of writing, that time gave me the ability to step back from the situation and act with purpose. As I took a moment to reread what I wrote, I realized that for the first time in my life, I was being vulnerable. And to my surprise, I liked the way it felt. I promised myself that I would continue to open my heart to friends and family and to capture every subsequent step in our journey for the world to read.

"When I entered Charlie's Room, she was sleeping very peacefully, it is such a relief to see her. Some of the partial burns on her chin are healing really well and her face looks beautiful. The OR docs and nurses washed Charlie's hair, she looked so clean and comfortable (not sure how), but she did. I gently touched her forehead and she opened her eyes. She saw me smile. She smiles softly and goes back to sleep. She was still under sedation from her surgery, so today we did not communicate very much, I just sat next her, turned on the music and just looked at her for the next two hours in silence, just thinking about our unforgettable memories, our boys and also trying to imagine what our new life is going to be."

—Excerpt From Journal Entry September 24, 2021

CHAPTER 6

Vows

As we faced this incredible challenge, regardless of the swirling schedule of Charlie's care, endless surgeries, and battles at every turn, there was one thing at the center of it all: the love that Charlie and I shared. There wasn't a moment when I didn't want to be at her bedside, comforting her, showing her support, and making sure she knew how loved she was and always would be. I quickly learned so much about our love through the tragedy we'd endured. It wasn't conditional. It wasn't based on an exchange of things we did for one another or our family. Our love was pure, everlasting, indelible. Sometimes it still ripped at me to think about the way I acted *before*. It was beginning to dawn on me that my behavior may have made Charlie feel like my love for her was heavily based on her actions; there were things I believed I deserved and that she should provide. Yet, through this tsunami of pain and suffering, I came to realize that, to me, Charlie will always be the perfect woman. She would be the Charlie I met with her short, spunky blond hair, dancing and laughing with abandon, caring for our children with all of her heart, and loving me endlessly despite my shortcomings. But she would also be Charlie the Survivor; the Warrior who fought fire and won. She continued to take my breath away each and every time I saw her. So much of me wanted to take her in my arms and hold her; to squeeze her tight, to kiss her lips, put my forehead against hers and breathe with her, but physical touch like that wasn't possible. Instead, through brief, gloved caresses of her forehead, running my fingers through her hair, and rolling my chair close to her head so I could whisper into her ear, I was able to show her the affection she deeply needed to receive, and I deeply needed to give.

With this permeating, layered love continuing to take shape between Charlie and me, things were developing in the outside world that caused me to think deeply about my life and my own relationship to the world around. As I continued to write daily, the journal began to pick up steam and gained hundreds of followers each day and news was starting to travel, women I didn't know would come up to me in the grocery store or at our local coffee place. They'd often say things like, "You must be so lonely, would you like to grab coffee?" or "This must be so hard on you. Maybe we can get a drink and talk about it?" This was never something I'd imagine happening, and it made me aware of a truth I'd not yet faced. The devil *always* tries to slither in and tempt you when you're at your lowest.

The more I thought about it, the more I realized how taboo this topic is. No one talks about the fact that when a strong couple, deeply in love and unshakably committed to one another, goes through something like this, their sex life will disappear for an undetermined amount of time. As a caregiver, I know this and have become comfortable with the fact that this is a long, winding road to recovery and our intimacy will trickle back over a period of years. After all, it's not just about Charlie getting out of the hospital, then in and out of rehab and back home. It's about Charlie's process of accepting her new and beautiful body and our shared journey toward discovering one another again. I never had any fear that I would stray, however, I also knew that I am a man with biological needs that I would have to contend with, and that fight would get harder as the devil does his work.

In my heart, I wanted to do something official to show Charlie what being on this healing journey alongside her meant to me. I wanted to show her that our love would continue to evolve over the time it took her to heal and that there was no rush. There was no danger that I would stray. All of this was about our family. It was about our marriage. I wanted to make sure that if she had any worries about me and my physical needs, that she'd never have to think about it. I wanted her to be able to put all her focus on healing, knowing that my love was selfless and that she could lean on me for anything, always.

Being Catholic, I knew there were a few steps I could take to create a sense of ceremony around the act of committing myself to celibacy. I decided to take a personal vow of chastity, to hold myself to a even higher standard than my marriage vows, so I turned to St. Thomas Aquinas's prayers:

The Prayer to St. Thomas Aquinas for Purity

Chosen lily of innocence, pure St. Thomas,

who kept chaste the robe of baptism,

and became an angel in the flesh after being girded by two angels,

I (we) implore you to commend me (us) to Jesus, the Spotless Lamb,

and to Mary, the Queen of Virgins.

Gentle protector of my (our) purity, ask them that I (we),

who wear the holy sign of your victory over the flesh,

may also share your purity,

and after imitating you on earth

may, at last, come to be crowned with you among the angels. Amen.[1]

As I read these prayers aloud, my body relaxed, and my heart felt rooted. I could feel God's steady presence as if His hands were on my back and he was whispering *This burden is mine now.*

---

1   https://www.knightsoftheholyeucharist.com/angelic-warfare-confraternity-petitions-for-chastity-prayer-download/

"This experience has transformed my mind, heart and soul in a very short period of time, but I also know this journey has just started."

—**Excerpt From Journal Entry September 14, 2021**

CHAPTER 7

Septic

As time slid by, I was beginning to recognize that some days would be much harder than others. On some days, I breezed through the time before I was able to go see Charlie, busying myself with work and chores. On other days, I struggled to drag myself out of bed, wallowing in pain that threatened to drown me. As hard as I'd try to rally, it took all my effort to do the smallest of things. I tried to be patient with myself on those days—but sometimes that patience wouldn't come.

On one such morning, I couldn't find any peace whatsoever. No matter where I went in the house, what I did, or what I thought about, my heart was crushed by sadness so heavy, I could hardly tug myself out from under it. All I wanted to do was go and see Charlie, so when it was finally time, I raced to the hospital, speeding well past the 70 mile per hour speed limit on Interstate 64 for the nearly two-hour drive, flung my car into a parking spot, threw open my door, and raced through the hospital doors as they slid open. I steeled myself as tears pricked the back of my eyes. I was having a hard time keeping the pain and fear where it needed to be—locked tight in the corner of my mind, far away from my heart.

When I finally reached Charlie's side, she was in good spirits. She was preparing for that day's surgery, waiting for the surgeon to come in and see her. I sat at her bedside and showed her videos of the boys. We chatted about the evening before, how the boys had been, and what was going on at home that day. As we talked and scanned through photos, I couldn't help but notice I had relaxed and that the feeling of pain that seemed to consistently be with me had slowly passed. It was all because of her. Charlie was my safe space; she was my home. And no matter what negative emotions threatened to take over, Charlie kept them at bay.

We were still scrolling through photos when the surgeon strolled into Charlie's room to ask how she was doing. Before she could muster an answer, the surgeon placed himself in front of her monitor—his brow furrowed. He reached into his pocket for his phone. After he punched several numbers into his calculator, he turned to me and said, "I need to go get someone smarter than me. I'll be back."

I leaned forward and touched Charlie's head.

Don't worry, my love.

Soon, the surgeon came back with another gentleman whose whitecoat nametag read "Head of Cardiology, VCU." They both pulled up the calculators on their phones and began tapping away. They finally looked up at each other and nodded their heads in agreement.

"What are you calculating?" I asked.

The surgeon responded, "Something is odd. We're looking at these monitors here and Charlie's heart is pumping blood satisfactorily, but the pressure on the capillary blood vessels is very weak, so we are trying to figure out what is going on. Normally, this is a strong indication that the patient is in septic shock."

I knew what that meant.

Major infection.

They warned us about this.

Of course, I frantically grabbed for my phone and tapped "Septic Shock" into the search engine.

Bad idea.

My limbs tingled as I processed the words on the page: "Fifty percent fatal." I clenched Charlie's rosary that had been blessed by Pope Francisco, pressed it to my heart, and prayed for God to protect her. Charlie closed her eyes as tears poured over her lids. She was brave, but she was also scared.

That was the first time I contacted Father Nick, the priest of the parish right next to the hospital, which is the former Cathedral of Richmond. He walked into our room within 20 minutes of my phone call and wasted no time. I shot up out of the chair next to Charlie and offered it to him. He sat down and leaned over the bed rail. I could hardly watch as he gave Charlie her last rites also known as the Anointing of the Sick.

Through this anointing may the Lord in his love and mercy help you with the grace of the Holy Spirit. Amen.

As Father Nick sat with Charlie, every ounce of hope left my body. I was an empty being, cavernous, void of anything resembling positive thought. Our luck was gone, my faith was shaken. I felt nothing but the cold, jagged edges of despair. Thoughts burst through my mind as I tried to process the certain horror I believed would soon befall us.

What happens when Charlie dies?

Do I sell everything and go back to Brazil with the boys?

No, I can't do that.

Do I ask my mom to move here and raise the kids with me?

No.

That's not fair to her.

I can't do this myself.

If she dies, do I remarry?

I could never do that.

I will never love someone like I love Charlie.

I can't do this alone.

I can't do this alone.

I can't do this alone.

I continued to clutch the rosary as Father Nick stood and motioned for me to join him in the hallway.

Once alone, he touched my arm and said, "It is important that you allow yourself to feel the pain of suffering in your heart. Do not just keep the pain in your head, because if you allow the pain to get into your heart, you will become one with Christ."

In that moment, his advice didn't penetrate my mind, but it comforted my soul. It gave me the strength to focus on Charlie's emotional wellbeing as we waited for news on her infection.

Thankfully, the news eventually was good.

It took me two or three weeks to come up with my own interpretation of what Father Nick said to me on that fateful day. To me, his words meant that whenever any negative feeling comes, instead of fighting and suppressing it, allow it to come in, embrace it even, and let it run its course so that it can make its way out. In allowing these feelings to do so, you leave room for Christ's love. For the longest time, that was not an option for me. I couldn't overcome the fear and negative thoughts, so I simply shoved them down. But Father Nick's words truly spoke to my spirit. I knew I had to learn to process my emotions and to nudge myself to focus on the present. After all, that was where I was needed most.

"Charlie is well aware of your efforts and love towards us, and she is beyond grateful and humbled by it. Please continue your prayers and positive thoughts, it is working."

—Excerpt From Journal Entry September 13, 2021

CHAPTER 8

Softening

Despite my love for Charlie, my ability to be there for her, and the resolve I had shown, I began to realize I had a long way to go. In that first week, I noticed myself pushing through anger over dozens of things.

How did this happen?

Why did this happen?

Who was responsible?

What could I have done?

Why wasn't I there?

Why hadn't I focused on loving Charlie better?

Now—now is the time to love her better, more tenderly.

Now.

In this space of grieving, I began to see the effects of my lack of compassion and kindness over the years. I was now in a place where I would need to suppress the hard, severe parts of myself and soften to everything around me. This was vital if I was going to get myself and my family through this in one piece.

The hardest thing for me to accept was the fact that we needed help. Yes, my mom would stay with us for as long as possible, so I had some help with the kids, but that didn't mean we had it all together. There was no way it was sustainable to have my mom who doesn't speak English be holding things down at home with the two kids, each of whom had schedules to maintain. Yet, despite people pushing to help, it was the last thing I wanted to allow in.

Charlie's mom friends were the first to push hard to help us with everything from meals to money, and this should have felt like a warm hug. Yet, in my altered reality, it felt like a stab to the heart. I felt ashamed. Immediately when they launched the Facebook page, they called me to ask if they could launch a GoFundMe and a Meal Train. As someone who based his self-worth on his success and accomplishments, I couldn't accept that we were now begging for food and money. I never wanted anyone to think we couldn't afford to feed ourselves or to pay for Charlie's treatment. That thought alone was enough to make me sick to my stomach, but my feelings didn't matter. I called Charlie's best friend to urge the group to hold off in asking for food and money on our behalf. "We are more than fine!" I exclaimed.

"André," said Charlie's friend, "It takes a village, and we are bringing that help to you. I'm sorry but you're going to accept this, Charlie would be doing this for any of us, we are doing it for her!

As much as it stung at the time, I was able to find deep gratitude for this conversation. We needed help. And I needed to find a way to accept that help. More importantly, on this journey, I had to learn to redefine what made me a person of value.

Being a father was something I always wanted, but I wasn't properly prepared to handle—especially the way Charlie believed parenting should look. My father was someone who loved me in his own way. A strict disciplinarian, he taught me how to be a man, and that started from a young age. He was someone that demanded a lot. He was someone who patted me on the back when I did something good and gave me hell when I did something bad. I saw my role as a parent as one where I'd provide guidance and discipline. I was hard hearted as a dad, just like I was as a husband at times. Charlie called me out on it few times over the years.

You have a cold, black heart.

In truth, I lacked empathy. When you don't have empathy, you can be mean—even cruel. That was me. For every bit of warm, sweet love Charlie provided, I provided my own stiff version of love. Little things triggered this ugly side of me often. For example, London had a certain toothpaste he never liked to use because it was too minty. He said it burned his mouth.

Anytime he complained about the toothpaste I would say to him, "London, stop whining. Brush your teeth."

He would start to cry.

I would toughen up even more.

I'd say, "You are a man and men don't cry."

He'd sob.

"I can give you a reason to cry if you really want one," I'd hiss through clenched teeth.

I had a lot to learn.

Just four years old, London didn't ask much about her whereabouts for a while. I was told that should be a relief because it just meant we were doing a good job keeping his routine mostly the same so at first he didn't notice a big difference. My mom hadn't gone back to Brazil, so she stepped right in to provide that nurturing, motherly figure for him. But now, as time was passing, I knew I was going to have to tell London that something was very wrong with Charlie, but I couldn't imagine doing so without Charlie by my side. She was the one who gave warm hugs and rubbed his back when he was sick or sad. She ruffled his hair when he was silly. She kissed skinned knees and sang him to sleep when nights were long. She loved him with the strength of a warrior.

Wanting to prepare myself, I made an appointment with a child psychologist who coached me on how to approach London.

Julien was too little to understand, but I'd sit him with us while we spoke, so it felt like the family unit was present.

On the day I decided to tell London, I went into his room and sat on the floor while he sat on his bed.

"London," I said softly, placing my hand on his knee. "You know mommy hasn't been home for a while, right?"

He nodded.

"Well, mommy got a big boo-boo and has to stay with the doctor, but she's okay."

He looked me in the eyes and said, "Okay ... but I miss her."

"I do too," I said, and opened my arms. London climbed down from the bed and nestled himself between my arms as I rested my chin on his head. I breathed in his scent—Burt's Bees Lavender shampoo. In that moment, I felt it. My heart became soft.

"I am the husband who didn't it help with the house chores. I am the husband who was always too busy with work to spend time with the kids. I am the husband who expected a home cooked meal for lunch and dinner. I am the husband who does not do his own laundry. I am the husband who would say hurtful things to my wife. I am the husband who has made his wife cry with my words. I am the husband who has become angry over petty things. I am the husband who would complain about the kids' mess. I am the husband who thought that I deserved to lay on the sofa after dinner and not help clean up because I worked so hard. I am the husband who refused to do better because I was too busy to bother. I am the husband without any empathy toward anyone. I am the husband who expected my wife to take care of the kids full time, help me with our business, clean the house, cook amazing meals and be happy and grateful to have me … I am so blessed to have a second chance to make it right. I am very grateful for God's grace, and I pray that he gives me the strength to change my ways."

—Excerpt From Journal Entry December 6, 2021

CHAPTER 9

A New Kind of Love

As I sat in the chair next to Charlie's hospital bed watching her sleep, I fought back the tears just wishing I could have Charlie back with me in our home, with our family, where she belonged. More than a month had passed since I told the boys about Mommy's "boo-boo" and we were settling into a routine that kept me endlessly busy and constantly running.

Now, more than ever, I appreciated Charlie's role as a mom—the 3 a.m. feedings, getting hardly any sleep, getting the kids ready in the morning, doing the laundry, tidying the house, running errands, cooking dinner, giving the kids a bath at night, and managing to spend some quality time with all of us in between. All these things are so hard for me to manage, even with my mom living with us. Yet, Charlie always seemed to breeze through it. In her rare moments of frustration, she'd vent to me, but it always fell on deaf ears. Or, on my worst days, with a snide, hurtful retort. I could never understand how the life she was living could lead to any kind of measurable, legitimate stress.

I can't believe how wrong I had been.

I leaned back in my chair staring at the silly spider Halloween decoration that had been stuck on the front of her glass box of a room. Charlie loved Halloween and always decorated the house, making it feel silly and spooky, which the boys loved. Now, here she was, locked in this room as I did my best to attempt the impossible; fill the role of Charlie at home. Regrets stabbed at me like a thousand needles pricking me all at once. I held my stomach and closed my eyes. The feelings of pain and shame were so visceral.

As I tried to calm myself, I remembered a few months ago, walking into the house at six o'clock one evening, and dinner wasn't yet ready.

Julien was whining.

Toys were strewn about the living room.

London was on the edge of a tantrum.

The kitchen was a mess.

The dining table had nothing on it but the remnants of an art project.

I didn't think to ask Charlie how her day went. I didn't care to greet her with a hug and a kiss. Instead, I sighed, "Charlie, I can't believe the state of things in here and that a hot meal isn't on the table. I've worked so hard all day and I come home to nothing ready for me and a house torn apart. What have you been doing all day?"

Her body tensed.

"You know what, André," she said, her face red, "If you want a hot meal, maybe you should just make it yourself."

Anger rose from my chest, white hot as she left the room to compose herself. I couldn't believe I was being treated this way after all I'd done for the family that day, that month, that year.

Soon, Charlie returned to the kitchen to begin cooking. I sat on the couch responding to emails on my phone, annoyed by the sound of cabinet doors opening and closing and plates and silverware hitting the counter. Charlie strained to talk to me from the kitchen. "Listen, London and another kid ran into one another at school today while playing tag, so he has a bump on his forehead."

I didn't respond.

"The school called so I had to run down there and sign an accident report."

I didn't respond.

She gathered the boys and put them each in their seats, then hustled out of the kitchen to bring my plate to the table and called me over.

As I pulled my chair out, Charlie asked, "Could you grab the ketchup from the refrigerator?

I didn't respond.

I was still mindlessly scrolling through my phone, now reading back through texts from the day.

"I could use a little bit of help, André," she said firmly while preparing to feed Julien.

I didn't respond.

The frustration in Charlie's tone matched what I was feeling too. But in that state—the state I lived in *before*—I couldn't see past myself. How could Charlie be annoyed in the least? This was the formula we purposefully set up. She would stay at home and take care of the kids while I worked to grow our businesses and pay the bills. Before we started out on this venture, we both saw each other's roles as important, but as time went by, bitterness set in on both sides. At the end of the day, I was ready to dive onto the couch and put my feet up before digging into my dinner. I never stopped to consider that Charlie had been waiting somewhere between nine and 12 hours to just get a small break. I was incapable of seeing her side because, over time, I had developed the unshakeable notion that my job was superior to hers.

Now I stared at Charlie, her eyes fluttering as she slept, and I was reminded of that moment with London on my lap and how I buried my nose into his hair as we hugged. That softening had continued to send ripples through my life, and as I watched Charlie sleep, the regrets continued to prick at me. I knew deep down that the one thing that would have made our arrangement seamless was the one thing that I lacked empathy. Charlie would have given anything for me to understand how demanding it is being a stay-at-home mom. Yet, I was so determined to make her understand the pressure I was under to provide for our family financially that I ignored all she provided. In retrospect, I realized that only half of that equation panned out to be fair. Not only did Charlie care for our children all day every day, but she also made sure I had lunch and dinner, did the chores around the house, made us all feel heard and loved, and even helped with the marketing for our businesses. And, unlike mine, her responsibilities did not stop at 6 p.m. She was on duty way after bedtime because that was when she'd get the chores finished up, and once her head hit the pillow, she was still on call. She'd have to wake anytime one of the boys needed something in the night; be it a glass of water, a nightlight switched on, one last kiss. I always assumed Charlie should be grateful that she didn't have to worry about the finances, yet she had more on her plate than I'd ever understood.

New and different ideas were emerging for me every day now, and as my mind bounced from thought to thought, I sat up in the lounge chair next to Charlie and started to tap search terms into my phone.

Stay at home moms.

Worth.

Value.

I wondered what kind of wage a stay-at-home mom would earn if we were to try and calculate such a thing, A little trolling on Google said the updated figure could be estimated at more than $180,000 a year. In truth, having done Charlie's job (with help) for more than a month, I had to admit that figure felt low.

After hours of wrestling with myself over the lack of gratitude I'd shown Charlie over the years, she began to stir. My face must have betrayed my feelings because she looked deep into my eyes and mouthed, "Are you okay?"

I was caught by surprise when she asked me this. My internal monologue was running at a mile per minute. I wanted to reach out and hug her. I wanted to collapse over her and sob, apologizing for all the ways I'd taken her for granted. I wanted to beg for her forgiveness. But as I looked into her eyes, I saw something I now recognized; something that I'd previously been unable to conjure: compassion.

I met her eyes, offering her the same.

In that moment, something clicked. It was as if our souls were recognizing one another the same way they had during those early conversations over romantic dinners. That gushing, heart-racing, indelible love was so present. God knows how much I wanted to tell her all my thoughts and worries and feelings. Charlie had always been there for me when I was stressed or struggling with something, and she always knew the right thing to say to make me feel better. Now, as I felt some of the worst pain since the accident itself, I yearned for my best friend and confidant to support me. But my heart knew better. As she gazed at me, sleepy-eyed and worried, it was my duty to look past myself and give Charlie what she needed most; comfort and reassurance.

I reached forward and caressed her forehead, "I'm fine, love. I promise."

Then I changed the subject.

I am well aware that Charlie's road to recovery won't be easy, I know that her pain will be unbearable, and her spirits may not always be positive or strong, and her psychological scars will take a long time to heal. I know how much sadness and pain our life will experience in the next few years, but I pray that God in his infinite mercy gives us the strength, hope, and drive to keep it going.

—Excerpt From Journal Entry, October 3, 2021

CHAPTER 10

ICU Syndrome

Every once in a while, I reflected over how much my life had changed. Once at a desk all day, barely looking away from my work, I was now living a largely transient life, driving back and forth to the hospital each day, two hours each way. Yes, I was also juggling the boys, managing our family's schedule, and working to keep our businesses running smoothly, but all those things were stuffed into the little bits of time I had between drives and visits with Charlie. My time in the car became sacred, it was my space to make phone calls I hadn't gotten to during the day, listen to enriching podcasts about mindfulness, or even just zone out in silence, letting the familiar sights and sounds of the trip lull me into some semblance of calm.

Our situation was dynamic—I never knew what exactly I would encounter when I reached her side. Now, nearly a month into her time in the ICU, things had begun to change. With all the medication Charlie was on, sometimes she had adverse reactions. In the past week I'd notice that she sometimes seemed miles away, staring off into space, her mind clearly busy. I'd get her attention and offer a smile and she'd smile back, but I could tell she was somewhere else. Something was troubling her, and I couldn't tell what exactly it was.

As days passed, I would arrive sometimes to find her crying— then the begging began. *She wanted to go home.*

"André, please. They're trying to kill me," whispered.

"Who is trying to hurt you?" I asked, confused.

"My nurse, Joe. He's been hitting me. Please, I need help. He's going to kill me."

One thought, and one thought only took hold: *I'm going to have to kill someone.*

Then I took a breath and began to think logically. We'd worked with Joe for weeks and he was always kind, respectful, and helpful. I'd never sensed anything about him that caused me to worry about having him around my wife. There had to be an explanation.

I paced the hallway until I found Joe, approached him and said, "Look, I'm really sorry to have to ask, but Charlie says you've been hurting her. What's been happening when I'm not here?"

Joe tucked a pen into the pocket of his scrubs as he responded, "Yeah, Charlie has had a rough day. I'm sure you've noticed lately that she's a little off?"

"Yes, she's seemed distracted a lot of the time," I said.

"This is an unfortunate side effect of being in the ICU for so long—it's called ICU Syndrome. Patients begin to hallucinate due to many factors."

"The meds. . ." I started.

"Yes, the meds, sleep deprivation from around-the-clock testing, and even urinary tract infections. All these things contribute to hallucinations that can be disturbing to patients. Please know, this happens to about 90 percent of ICU patients. It know it's awful to witness and that you're in a helpless place, but I promise, this is temporary."

Now that I was able to recognize ICU Syndrome, I could tell when Charlie was beginning to spiral into her terrifying fantasies. I'd arrive and she'd become hysterical the moment she saw me, begging for me to come to her side. Her eyes wild, she'd whisper to me things like:

"They're trying to steal my baby."

"My grandmother is here standing over me, can't you see her?"

"There are tunnels beneath the hospital."

"They're in the tunnels, they're coming for me."

"I need help."

"Please, please."

"Help."

I would stand by her head and sing to her softly, as if my beacon of strength were a helpless little girl afraid of monsters in her mind. She loved my fingers in her hair and would relax beneath my touch, then finally drift off to sleep. There, wrapped in her dreams, she was safe.

As I watched her sleep, I'd let my own pain come. I'd wonder if she'd lost her mind. I'd obsess over the possibility that she may never return to me. I'd curse the helpless feeling I was constantly forced to endure. I wanted my wife back with me, feeling her fingers interlaced with mine. Yet, all I could do was caress the few parts of her body that had not been ravaged by flames and sing sweet lullabies in Portuguese to help keep the hallucinations at bay.

We were fortunate that ICU Syndrome didn't overwhelm Charlie for long. With a few changes in medications and other small adjustments, she was back to herself within a week and a half. Like most things as patients heal, the hallucinations did come back to haunt Charlie once more when, in the OR, they used a drug she didn't tolerate well, but that time the torture was short lived. That was the thing we've come to learn about the cadence of healing: two steps forward, one step back.

"[Her surgeon] officially announced to Charlie that he would be shaving her hair on October 19, the day of her first CEA application. Charlie just looked at him and said, 'Ok, as long my hair grows back.' I told her he said it will."

—Excerpt From Journal Entry, October 10, 2021

CHAPTER 11

Shaved

Watching your loved one endure such unspeakable pain and so many horribly painful procedures gives you with a feeling of helplessness I cannot explain. You look on and wish to do something, anything, to make the pain stop, but you can't. You are eternally trapped in a cycle of watching and willing it to be over. Some of the worst things to witness, however, have very little to do with medical procedures and watching your loved one struggle through. Sometimes it has to do with the stripping of humanity that happens to all patients, especially to those in long-term care.

When Charlie's surgeon announced that he would be shaving her head On October 19, my stomach flipped. He explained that he'd have to shave her head in the operating room to get access to the skin on her scalp, which he'd harvest a piece of to use for upcoming grafting procedures. As the surgeon spoke,

I Charlie nodded calmly then said, "As long as it grows back, I'm fine with it."

Charlie was stronger than I'd ever imagined she'd be; she had endured so much but I feared this would take a toll on her, causing a swift jab she wouldn't see coming. I obsessed over it happening and found myself picturing her coming out of the procedure depressed and deeply discouraged. I knew I had to trust that Charlie would be honest with me about how she was feeling, but I feared deep down that losing her hair would feel to her like she was being stripped of her femininity. That seemed like a sharp blow on top of everything she had already been through.

As the date approached, I my mind raced, searching for ways I might be able to help. Then, it dawned on me, I might be able to have the surgery staff save Charlie's hair and I could have a wig made from it. I began to do research and reaching out to well-known wig makers, but I quickly realized that this wouldn't be a possibility—apparently a wig maker needed four heads' worth of hair to make a single wig. I had pictured being able to give Charlie the incredible gift of her sense of self, but there was no way to make it happen the way I envisioned.

I ended up making the decision to talk to Charlie's core group of best friends to see if they had any ideas. It turned out that one of them had a close family friend who is a world renowned a wig maker who makes wigs for Broadway plays. As they always do, without fail, Charlie's friends jumped into action and began laying out plans to have the perfect wig made. As the plans took shape, my worries about the procedure began to disappear. I finally felt like I was able to control something and bring my wife some joy she so desperately needed.

On the day of the procedure, I anxiously awaited Charlie being wheeled back into her room. Although I knew she'd seemed okay with the shaving happening, I couldn't shake the thought that the experience would rattle her. I closed my eyes.

Charlie's wide eyes staring into mine.

Tears rolling down her cheeks.

My hand caressing her head.

Leaning close.

Whispering into her ear, I love you.

When the time finally came for me to see Charlie following the procedure, I couldn't believe my eyes. She was smiling, looking up at me with sleepy eyes. Her head was shaved down close to the scalp and there was a bandage covering the area where tissue had been harvested. The tears I expected never came. Instead, Charlie seemed to feel relief, now free of the matts that had plagued her hair since the accident. As I approached her, her smile broadened.

"You look beautiful, my love."

"Thank you," she mouthed.

Through all my fear about Charlie's femininity being stolen, I never stopped to think about the fact that tragedy causes a cascade of reprioritization. I was so caught up in yet another thing being stolen from Charlie that I never stopped to think that she might really have found peace within herself about certain things. At this point, healing for Charlie was about endurance, strength, and putting in the work to get herself home to her family. She truly had no concern about little things—like hair that would grow back. I was beginning to see that healing was all about the give and take, the push and the pull. It wasn't about clinging to the past or obsessing about the future. It was about living in gratitude firmly planted in the here and now.

Eventually, the beautiful wig Charlie's friends commissioned arrived. She tried it on, and it looked perfect, allowing her to recapture a small sliver of the past. After wearing it for just a few moments, Charlie slid the wig off and handed it back to me. Although she had deep gratitude for her friends' hard work, it seemed Charlie was more comfortable embracing the point in her healing where she found herself. Part of focusing on healing was embracing our new and beautiful life. That began with the shedding of skin, the shaving of hair, and the willingness to fight with valor.

"Initially [my journals] were a form of daily update on Charlie's condition to close family members and friends. It has now evolved into an X-ray view of my mind and experiences as a caregiver and advocate. Please know that I am choosing to be vulnerable and open about my feelings for two reasons. One, I really hope that anyone reading these journals can be inspired or validated in how they feel in the face of crises or trials. Two, I want to let everyone know that it is ok to be sad but is also important to find the light out of the darkness. After all, to have light, darkness must exist."

—Excerpt From Journal Entry October 29, 2021

CHAPTER 12

White Lies

It was like walking a tightrope every time I stepped into that hospital. In Charlie's room, I'd learned to be nurturing and calm, showing her all the love in my heart. When I stepped out of her room, I knew I needed to be strong and assertive so that I could be the fiercest activist and protector she had ever known.

On this journey, I was beginning to learn shocking, yet unavoidable truths about the American Healthcare System. Yes, hospitals exist to care for and, ultimately, heal patients. But the system is far more complicated and nuanced than you can imagine. Policies are in place, practices are established, and whether we like to admit it or not, cash is king. When you enter a hospital, you become a patient, and as a loved one, you have two choices—become an advocate or accept your beloved's fate.

Of course, I chose the former.

Charlie's care was so dynamic that I had to remain on high alert at all times. Between daily surgeries, grafting of the lab-grown skin, drying sessions to help the new skin properly take to her body, the risk of infection, and monitoring her levels and the care administered, I was thrust into a world where I quickly had to become an expert in the medical field. I poured over data, kept up-to-date on the most recent research on every procedure and its risks, and jumped into action anytime I noticed symptoms that the staff either ignored or played off as insignificant. That wouldn't cut it for my warrior of a wife, so I made a promise. I would use every ounce of my strength to fight for optimal care.

My first major opportunity to advocate for Charlie was over the medication Oxycodone. Charlie has been sensitive to opioids since I've known her. She had always had a standing prescription for Oxycodone for her Rheumatoid Arthritis, but she rarely took it because it made her feel too drowsy.

One day early on, the nursing staff gave her Oxycodone mixed with some other medication, and in less than 30 minutes Charlie began to go in and out of consciousness. Then, without warning, her blood pressure dropped enough to set the alarm off, catalyzing a flurry of activity in the room.

The nurses scrambled trying to wake Charlie, working to get her to focus on anything at all. In desperation, they then fumbled for a button that made the bed vibrate violently. Apparently, this was a technique they used to provoke various responses in patients, in her case they were trying to normalize her blood pressure. I flinched as Charlie's raw, aching body shook with the bed. I couldn't believe what I was seeing.

Not afraid to speak up on Charlie's behalf, I broke through the chaos and calmly said to the nurses, "I feel like there is a connection between the Oxycodone and her pressure dropping. She's had issues with that medication in the past."

Ignoring me, they continued trying different maneuvers to help balance her levels. Her pressure finally normalized about 20 minutes later. The nurses and doctors acted puzzled, as if they had no clue what possibly could have caused her pressure to drop. But I knew.

And I tried to tell them.

The next day as I sat with Charlie, the nurses came in to administer meds. Of course, mere moments later, the same thing happened again. There was rushing, poking, prodding, maneuvering, and violent shaking until her pressure normalized.

This time, I was a little more aggressive when I said, "Charlie has reacted poorly to Oxycodone in the past. How can I request that the hospital not give her Oxycodone anymore?"

The nurse promised me she'd make a note in Charlie's chart, but the note didn't seem to do much at all; certainly nothing consistent. On some days the staff obeyed and kept the Oxycodone away, and on other days they'd administer it, sending Charlie into a spiral that always ended in nurses violently trying to rouse her. I couldn't make sense of what was going on. Was there a shift change would often mean my request fell on deaf ears. How was it that I was unable to get a medication that undeniably caused harm removed from my wife's care plan?

Over the weeks, I'd lost count of how many Oxycodone scares we had. I finally broke down and, choking back tears, begged the nurse we'd known the longest to help me.

She called me to her side and quietly said, "Look, I am going to give you a tip here. The only thing you can do to guarantee that your request goes across all shifts is to include Oxycodone as an allergy in her chart."

The nurse then agreed to help me add it to her allergy chart, thus ending my battle with Oxycodone for good. I gingerly held Charlie's hand in mine that night and promised her that I would forever be her soldier in this battle we'd been thrust into.

As much as I despised clawing my way through the battle over Oxycodone, it was the fight that made me realize what it would take to be her best advocate. I not only had to be impeccably informed, I also had to be willing to do whatever it took to receive the *right* care for Charlie—even if it meant telling a white lie.

"Patience is a virtue and not an easy one. I am so grateful for Charlie's amazing recovery, truly she has been remarkable; even her nurses agree on how remarkable she has been. But I also need to recognize that she is human and bad days will occur. Maybe God wants me to remain humble and not get too confident? It is not easy, and I am fighting so hard to not give in to fear, because by now I know the damage that fear can do to my spirit, and I don't want to leave my grateful state. Please pray for me to not give in to fear."

—Excerpt From Journal Entry November 9, 2021

CHAPTER 13

Vent

The first weeks and months in the hospital were spent locked in battle over a piece of equipment I came to despise: the trach. Shorthand for Tracheostomy Tube, a trach is a device that allows patients to breathe through a stoma (hole in the throat) with plastic fitted inside to protect the flesh from infection. The trach also comes with a collar that the patient must wear while the trach is inserted and attached to a ventilator.

Watching Charlie deal with the trach was one of the most wrenching parts of early recovery. Strong-willed and hungry for comfort, Charlie would try to pull at the tube, desperately trying to free herself from it. The ill-fitted collar would slip, causing abrasions on some of the only healthy skin she had left. Instead of customizing care to give Charlie comfort, the hospital delt with this by fitting her with cloth handcuffs that fastened to the rails of her bed so she couldn't move to tug, pull, or adjust. Seeing her this way ate at me, my heart yearning to free her as my mind wrestled with the fact that this was a necessary part of saving my Charlie's life.

This was when I began to learn even more about Standard of Care, a term that refers to guidelines that outline the appropriate care to be given to a patient for specific diseases and injuries. I immediately realized there was an inherent problem with Standard of Care procedures—namely, the fact that these standards mean that care isn't customized. Instead, care is tailored to the average person who succumbs to the illness or injury, completely disregarding the patient's individual needs. In part, this was why it had been so hard to get rid of the Oxycodone in Charlie's care plan; Oxycodone was a part of standard care for burn patients.

How could it be that every patient was bound by the same standards?

It seemed obvious to me that the demographics of burn victims would vary between patients. Gender. Ethnicity. Age. Medical history. Access to care. Height. Weight. But the medical world didn't see it that way. Since Charlie's Standard of Care was optimized for the "typical" burn victim; males much larger than Charlie and —the standard simply didn't align with Charlie's circumstances. This meant the standards for the cutting of the stoma, the fitting of the collar, all of it, had been created for a man nearly twice Charlie's size. So, on top of the agony Charlie was already in from being stuck on a ventilator, she was dealing with the unnecessary pain of being shackled to equipment that didn't fit.

In those early days, as she lay on the ventilator, I knew there had to be a way to make Charlie more comfortable. And, in my opinion, the easiest thing they could do was to downsize her collar.

I begged nurses.

I pleaded with doctors.

I hounded our case manager.

It all fell on deaf ears.

Adding to the pain of seeing Charlie cuffed and her skin breaking where the collar was rubbing, was witnessing the sheer torment forced upon those on a ventilator. With the trach inserted, Charlie was not only unable to eat, she also wasn't allowed to have any liquids due to the risk of aspiration. This was pure torture for Charlie who felt the anguish of unquenchable thirst as she lay in her bed hour after hour, day after day, the trach working to keep her oxygen levels stable. She'd try to mouth words to me; to get me to understand what she needed, but it was sometimes impossible for me to decipher what she was desperately trying to say. She would get frustrated. I would get frustrated. That was the name of the lip-reading game, which we were bound to. After all, you can't scribble on a notepad while cuffed to a bed, and the hospital was adamantly against us using a lip-reading app I had found.

Thankfully, Charlie's early time on the ventilator was short, however, the stoma and collar needed to remain in place so the doctors could easily access her airway. For the time being, we were able to remain grateful despite the scraping of the collar. Saying goodbye to the ventilator was cause for celebration.

I took a breath and exited my car in the hospital parking lot. The air was crisp as I quickly slipped my mask on and headed toward the door. Thanksgiving was looming, which added an edge to my pain. I wanted to be endlessly grateful that Charlie was alive; to relish the fact that we'd eventually be able to hold one another again. Yet, as the holiday season was set to begin, all I could do was grieve what we were all missing.

More and more, I was finding myself succumbing to an overwhelming feeling of *saudades*—a Portuguese word that refers to a deep emotional state of nostalgic or profound melancholic longing for something or someone that you care for or love. Moreover, it often carries a repressed knowledge that the object of longing might never be had again. It is the recollection of feelings, experiences, places, or events that once brought excitement, pleasure, and well-being, which triggers the senses and causes deep pain of separation from those joyous sensations. This was exactly what I was experiencing as I went through life without Charlie, which was punctuated by the anticipation of holidays. Though I had hopes that she would one day be back home with us, nestled right back into her space in the family, I couldn't help but continue to grieve. Things would never be the same again.

I headed up to the burn unit and suited up in a ritual I was now accustomed to. I scrubbed my hands carefully, pulled on gloves, and slipped myself into my suit, which zipped up covering my head and face. There was only a plastic window for me to gaze out of.

I stepped out of the changing room and headed to Charlie's room, the suit making swishing sounds as I walked. I stopped suddenly in front of the glass door to Charlie's room. Horror overcame me as I took in what I could never have fathomed. Charlie was back on the ventilator, the ill-fitted collar back around her neck. My heart sank as I tried to compose myself. I thought we'd left this awful machine behind us. I thought we were finished with this part of the healing journey. Yet, here it was, back to haunt us with the beeping and whirring noises that we'd since replaced with calming music.

The vision broke my heart, but that sadness quickly turned into anger. Before I even entered Charlie's room, I turned around and stormed down to the nurse's station. I felt like we'd just been kicked back a million steps. She had been off the vent for a month, so why was she back on it?

Having come to know me well, the nurses fully expected me to be upset. It was hard to control myself as I stormed up to the nurses' station and demanded answers.

Charlie has lost every ounce of autonomy she'd worked so hard to gain.

Why on earth does she need to be on the vent anyway?

Her oxygen saturation is better when she is off of it!

Who put these orders in?

Did Charlie have any say in this whatsoever?

No matter how loud I became or how animated I was, the nurses just stared back at me, reassuring me that these measures were necessary and that a doctor would be in to talk to us shortly.

I stomped back to Charlie's room and composed myself before slowly making my way inside. I stepped to her bedside and stared into her glassy eyes. She attempted a smile. I knew what a loss of independence that ventilator symbolized for Charlie. I knew how much this must have been hurting her. But she never complained. She never communicated her revolt. She was always so graceful in these situations, and I tried to let that be my guide.

I took deep breaths as Charlie motioned with her eyes. Here we were—back in the painfully familiar routine.

"I'm so thirsty," she mouthed. "Please."

I wanted to cry.

I softly repeated over and over, "I can't, Charlie. You know I can't."

"Please give me some water, André."

I steeled myself.

She pleaded with me, "Please, André, please."

I hesitated before going to the sink and filling a cup with water. I then reached for a washcloth, which I wetted and ran over her lips and tongue.

She begged for more.

I couldn't give her what she wanted.

Then she mouthed, "André, would you brush my teeth?"

"Of course," I responded softly. I reached over for the tiny swab and suctioning device I was allowed to use. She opened her mouth, and I ran the swab over her teeth and dabbed around her mouth with suction. As I worked, her eyes softened. I could feel her relaxing under this small act; an act that offered her a sliver of the dignity she deserved.

After I'd finished cleaning her teeth, Charlie drifted off to sleep. I prayed that she was able to find an escape in her dreams; to let sleep carry her far from this room somewhere safe. I hoped she was able to find herself in a swirl of distant memories, free to walk, dance, and play with the boys in fields of green.

As I paced the room, the hospital psychologist standing outside Charlie's room caught my eye. With Charlie asleep, I was able to excuse myself without revealing to her that I was upset. But the Psychologist saw it all over my face the second I walked out of the room.

Without skipping a beat, she said, "Anger is a normal response to fear and a loss of control, Andre, but you've got to keep it in check for Charlie."

"I'm sorry. I'm just so frustrated." Tears were now streaming down my face. "So many things seem to be going against us and I can't do anything about it!"

"I know," she responded. "Just breathe. Someone will be in to see you soon."

I was so broken at that point that I didn't even have the strength to ask questions, protest, or do much of anything at all. But the outrage welled up inside me. I wanted to kick and scream, to punch walls, to explode into a thousand pieces. Instead, I reminded myself to feel the pain in my heart and returned to Charlie's bedside.

Even lying in the bed hooked up to a myriad of machines, covered in bandages with a tube coming out of her throat, she was still my pillar of strength. Her light guided me in every step I took. I felt the deepest sadness for so many things. The excruciating pain she went through daily. The loss of independence. The fear and confusion she must have been feeling. The yearning to be with her boys. But I never felt pity. Not one time. Charlie is not a person you feel pity for. She is a force to be reckoned with. The strength she exuded brought me the comfort I needed to keep moving forward.

And my faith.

1 Peter 5:10, "After we have suffered, the God of all grace will restore, establish, and strengthen us." God promises that our suffering will ultimately be followed by Glory.

In the weeks that followed, I did what I had come to rely on as a means of comfort—research. I read dozens of medical papers, studies, and articles. If Charlie would have to have her airway remain open, I would find a way to make her more comfortable. I learned as much as I could about trach collars and why certain decisions were made regarding sizing. I compared sizes, discovered the exact difference between each, and learned where we needed to land to make things better for Charlie. I concluded that Charlie should be downgraded to a size six collar, which would not only make her far more comfortable, but would also speed up her journey toward being able not only to drink liquids and eat again, but to finally speak above a whisper. Of course, I yearned to hear Charlie's voice again, but this wasn't the only reason I wanted Charlie to be able to speak. I felt strongly that she was in dire need of psychiatric care and that we should prioritize her ability to interact with the hospital psychiatrist.

Research in-hand and now able to speak the language of this extremely nuanced medical procedure, I went to Dr. Bergin to plead my case. Standing in the hallway outside of Charlie's room, I explained to him how sad and despondent Charlie had become and how these feelings needed attention from a professional. "And she won't be able to get the help she needs if she is unable to talk," I added.

"André, right now, we are concerned about Charlie's life. We're not concerned with her psychiatric care."

I could hardly believe what I was hearing. I wanted to scream. I wanted to pull out every bit of research I'd done and shove it in his face, but he was so unmoving and rigid, I knew I wouldn't get anywhere with him, no matter how hard I tried. So, instead of pushing him harder, I thanked him for his time and devised a new plan.

Over the next few days, I pled my case to anyone who would listen. After talking to countless nurses, I decided to meet with the head of psychiatric care for the hospital. I shared my thoughts with her, explained the research I had done and what I understood to be true about trach collars, and begged for help, explaining how much Charlie was struggling emotionally. "Please, she is so depressed. I need your help. It would make such a difference if you'd to talk to Dr. Bergin about how important psychiatric care is."

"I agree with you. It is so important to care for a patient's mental health, but I can't go to Dr. Bergin and demand that he listens to me. He's the head of the burn unit, which means he has the ultimate say in what happens with Charlie's care."

I rubbed my forehead and calmed myself before I spoke. "So, you're telling me that, as the head of psychiatry of this hospital, you do not have the pull to tell another doctor that you require this change because you *need* your patient to be able to speak with you? I don't understand. In my eyes, the mind and body are equally important."

She pursed her lips, then continued, "André, that is a valid feeling, but I'm telling you, that's not how it works here."

I drew a breath

Although I hoped to move the needle, nothing I was saying or doing was making any kind of a difference. As the psychiatrist walked away, her heels clicking on the sterile floor, all I could do was look at Charlie through the glass. From there I could see the wound on her neck from the collar rubbing against her skin. I watched as she scrolled on her iPad, her brows knitted together in a way they never used to be. I had to be her warrior and search for one *yes* in a sea of endless *nos.*

My next tactic was to speak with the head of the ICU—the Medical Director—with whom I had a special bond. We spoke in Spanish, and I explained to him that I wanted Charlie downsized so she could speak to her psychiatrist. I explained the research I had done, quoted a few of my sources, and asked if he would speak with Dr. Bergin about the downsize. I watched as he hesitated to give me an answer.

Finally, he spoke, "I hear you and I understand your concerns. And, yes, my team is the one that performs the downsizing. However, this order must come from Dr. Bergin himself."

Another dead end.

I thanked him for his time and sat down in a chair adjacent to the nurse's station. I knew I had to figure out next steps, but I couldn't see where to go next. My mind was racing, sifting through everyone I'd met at the hospital so far, their credentials, and who might be able to help me. Having reviewed my research over and over, I knew my facts front, back, and sideways. Yet, no matter where I looked or who I spoke to, it appeared I'd receive the same answer; Dr. Bergin was the person who needed to make the call, and no one would even attempt to talk to him on Charlie's behalf. My mind buzzed with medical facts and personal tactics while my heart remained heavy.

With all the conversations I was having, it shouldn't have been a surprise to me that Dr. Bergin caught wind of what I was doing. He reached out and asked that I sit down with him to have a conversation about what was going on. Heading into the meeting, I felt hopeful. This was my chance to present the full body of my research to the one and only person who had the power to make the call. I got to the conference room early, opening my notebook and preparing to pull up research papers on my phone.

As I reviewed the pertinent information, Dr. Bergin breezed into the room and pulled up a chair across from me.

"Dr. Bergin, how are you?" I asked, reaching out my hand to meet his.

His handshake was firm.

His stance was rigid.

His face was flat.

"So," he began, "I hear you've been speaking to the staff about downsizing Charlie's trach. You and I have already spoken about this, André."

"I know we have, but I've done so much more research since then and I'd like to explain to you what I found and why I believe there is no reason she can't be downsized."

"Go ahead," Dr. Bergin responded, leaning back in his chair.

I pointed to the notes in my notebook and began to summarize for Dr. Bergin all the papers I had read, the science I'd delved into, and the truths I'd come to learn about trach collars. I made my case explaining how badly I needed Charlie to be able to communicate, how her mental health was struggling, and how the science proved the downsize was safe. Pointing to my phone I said, "Look, the research shows a size six trachea collar allows the patient to have a speaking valve put in and it provides enough space in case of emergency. The difference between a number six and a number eight is half of a millimeter in diameter, but the difference in quality of life for Charlie would be huge."

Dr. Bergin leaned forward and placed his hands on the table in front of him. He narrowed his eyes. "Look, research is one thing. Real life is completely different. You have no idea the risks Charlie will face if we downsize."

I stayed quiet, unsure what to say.

"So, if you feel good enough about your research to override my medical expertise, fine, you can sign a disclaimer and a waiver and I will downsize the collar on your wife. But at that point, if something happens in the OR and I cannot access her airways because of the size change, she will die."

At that thought, my heart began to race.

"Do you want to sign the waiver?" he asked.

"No." I said, crestfallen. "I'm sorry to be pushing so hard, but I am beyond frustrated. I want her to be able to speak. I want to be able to quench her thirst. I want so much for her …"

"I understand," he said, his voice softening. "Here is what I'll do. I commit to you that I will reevaluate her by next week and see if there is any chance we could downsize her without risk."

"I appreciate that," I said, choking back tears.

"If there is any way we can do it safely, I promise you, I will downsize Charlie's collar."

With a nod, Dr. Bergin left the conference room.

At that moment, a swirl of emotion overtook me. I had made a difference; I had gotten someone—*the* someone—to listen and promise me he'd reevaluate. But the feeling of joy was hampered by the feelings of fear I now wrestled with. Now alone in the conference room, I held my head in my hands, yearning for the days when death never crossed my mind.

"Great news," Dr. Bergin said as he walked into Charlie's room just one week later. "I conducted an examination this morning and it looks like we will be able to downsize Charlie's collar within the week."

Charlie was beaming with excitement while I was more reserved. Although I would do anything to increase Charlie's comfort levels, Dr. Bergin had given me a hard dose of reality. I hoped that he wasn't pushing things too fast just to appease me; he didn't seem like that kind of guy.

The next day, Charlie went in for her next skin grafting surgery, which was approximately five hours long. When the doctors put her under, her blood saturation started dropping, her oxygen levels falling all the way to 40%, which is remarkably low compared to the normal range of 95% or higher. The team jumped immediately into action, acting like she was going to code, even though they were unsure what was going on. They got the defibrillator ready, but thank God it was not necessary. It turned out she had a little bit of fluid on her left lung, which caused a partial collapse. That is why her saturation was low. To clear the fluid and restabilize her, they had to rush to do a fluid extraction, requiring them to use all the space the size eight collar had to offer.

Following the surgery, I sat by Charlie's side, praying with her as she found herself back on the ventilator once more.

When I looked up, Dr. Bergin was standing in the doorway. "See?" he said. "This is why we don't consider downsizing in cases like Charlie's. You need to hear me when I say that we will not be downsizing her until further notice."

This time, I heard him loud and clear.

"Our friends are holding a fundraiser for Charlie's medical bills at Patch Brewing Co. hopefully I will meet some of you there, and even if you can't come, you can bid on some incredible prizes, like a cruise and a hotel stay. This will be my first time back at Patch in public since the accident, I will do my best to hold my emotions in place, but forgive me if you see me crying, I just don't know how I will react being there with so many friends."

Excerpt from Journal Entry, November 13, 2021

CHAPTER 14

Patch

There were days when I'd wake with a pit in my stomach. Before even getting out of bed, I'd sit and wrestle with all the factors at play as we navigated this part of our journey. In moments like those, it was hard to separate all the disparate pieces of the massive puzzle that had become my life. Busyness with the boys became braided with piles and piles paperwork and flooding thoughts about Charlie and her various procedures, all of which were tangled up with decisions I'd have to make regarding Patch.

Patch began as a joint dream for Charlie and me—one that we shared with our business partner, Jon. We envisioned a place where families could come together and play. We pictured a place where you could gather and have a full day of fun. We imagined folks bringing their kids and letting them play on the sprawling, lush lawn. Adults would be able to choose from a wide selection of handcrafted beers to sip while their kids ran free. Not only that, but we'd even have an enclosed area where dogs could play. We talked about guests then settling down at a table with tired kids coloring on butcher paper table covers while the dog settled at their feet. They'd then order from a menu full of savory food, incorporating as many local ingredients as possible. When we talked about Patch, Charlie's eyes would sparkle. She had such big, beautiful dreams about how much joy it would add to our community.

Building a business, however, is different than dreaming. There are constant demands that pull you in dozens of directions all at once. Things become busy, priorities are set, and the work begins. For Charlie and me, this began our conflicts about what should happen as the business was being built and what our roles should be. Of course, this is what led to our fateful argument the night before the accident.

You should be there.

I'm there because you aren't.

You're leaving this all to Jon—it's not fair.

From my new perspective, it was becoming hard for me to accept the way I had behaved. I'd truly believed it was not my job to get my hands dirty and that I would better serve Patch from my office, dealing with the bank. The thought still plagued me. If I had been there, maybe, just maybe, Charlie's accident wouldn't have happened.

Now, my relationship with Patch was distant and complicated. The grand opening had come and gone when I was at Charlie's side during some of the most critical days early on in her recovery. Not only did I miss the opening, I hadn't been there at all since Charlie's accident. The first day was a massive success, bringing in more money than any of our other businesses, but it was also a place that had stolen so much.

To make matters more complicated, there was the legal side of things. As a part owner of the business, I was technically Charlie's employer when the accident happened. That meant I was locked in a legal battle over what happened, who was at fault, and how the matter could be resolved in court, or settled some other way. I wished I could make myself go to Patch, see its magic, and find the joy in something we'd worked so hard to build. Yet, this place that was meant to represent a beautiful, shared dream, now represented the nightmare our family was living.

As November approached, Charlie's friends began to galvanize to host a fundraising event. They planned a silent auction, donation stations, and portions of sales proceeds to go directly toward Charlie's medical bills. Without question, I was more than happy to offer up Patch as a location for the event. However, I'd be lying if I said I wasn't terrified to set foot there.

I hadn't been back to the brewery since the accident. In fact, I'd only seen pictures of it since it'd become operational. I tried picturing myself there, walking into the main building, then out into the fields where people were laughing and enjoying themselves, sipping cold beer in warm rays of sunshine. But anytime I thought about going, I felt sick. How could I not? At the very mention of Patch, there were images of Charlie walking into the building on that fateful morning with no idea what was to happen. I pictured her setting up to work. Plugging in the sander. Getting herself set up to sand the boards.

Flash.

Flames.

The fury of fire.

I was a strong man. I knew I could control my emotions. But this was different. I was beginning to learn what trauma was all about and the fact that it never truly goes away. It just sits there beneath your skin, waiting.

When the day came, every bone in my body begged me to stay home. I wanted to run far away; to avoid stepping foot on the property at all costs, but there was no way out. I had to go to the event and represent our family, showing our deep gratitude to Charlie's friends and our community. So, I strapped the boys into the car and drove the familiar path. The closer we got to Patch, the more violently my stomach flipped.

We pulled into the parking lot.

I looked up from the steering wheel.

The door she walked through, engulfed.

The gravel where she rolled.

The picnic table that she was seated.

Breathe.

I casually kept my eyes trained on the ground as I got the boys out of the car and watched them run to join their friends who were running around the baseball diamond. I was immediately greeted by friends and family, all of whom wrapped me in big hugs one by one. Charlie's best friend walked me around so I could see what they had put together for the auction. I stayed focused. I maintained tunnel vision. I didn't let my eyes drift. I couldn't believe what the women had put together. They had managed to get incredible prizes, like tickets for a cruise, family photo sessions, hotel stays, and more. As I looked at the items, a lump formed in my throat.

I miss Charlie.

I wish she was here.

I want to reach for her.

I want to hold her hand.

I cleared my throat and let Charlie's friends lead me to a group of people waiting to say hello. I was then swept into conversation for the better part of an hour, meeting local members of the Facebook group, catching friends up on Charlie's recovery, and sharing some stories from inside the hospital. I stayed focused on conversations. I let myself enjoy the distraction. I pushed thoughts about the accident aside. I relaxed.

Finally, during a lull in the conversation, I took a deep breath. Then another. And another. As my shoulders dropped and I took a sip of my ice cold, hoppy beer, I centered myself. Then I heard it.

Laughter.

I followed the sound, walking out from beneath the pavilion. Finally, slowly, I let myself experience my surroundings. The air was crisp. The sun was beaming down. Children were running in the fields giggling, playing games of tag. Dogs were wrestling in the dog park, letting out excited barks now and again. Groups of people were sipping beers and tossing beanbags, cheering one another on in long games of corn hole on the lawn. The bar area was packed—full of excited people chatting, sharing beers, and enjoying every moment. My heart swelled. Tears pricked the backs of my eyes. This was the exact vision Charlie and I had for this place. My breath caught in my throat, but the tears never came. Instead, a feeling of joy draped itself over my entire being.

As complex as things had become, I began to realize, the truth was simple. Patch wasn't a place that needed to represent the tragedy. Instead, it was possible for Patch to become a beacon of hope. Our community had come together to give us so much— now, they had a place to gather that was unlike anything our town had ever seen. It was a place for joy. It was a place for comfort. It was a place for fun. Most of all, despite everything that happened there, it was a place that managed to maintain a delicious feeling of love. In so many ways, it felt like home.

Actually ... it felt like Charlie.

"Love, imagine when a little boy, takes his dog to get a vaccine at the vet and the dog looks at him in terror of the needle. Could the little boy explain to his dog that the vaccine is going to protect him to not get sick, would the dog understand? No, because the kid and the dog don't speak the same language. Well, we are like the dog, and God is like the kid on this story. Even though Jesus was human, Father God is not, and His understanding is different than ours.

"There is no way to understand why he would allow tragedy to happen to anyone. I can try to understand that tragedy like this does happen, and that God may use this horrific event to inspire, and give hope to a lot of people, but only He knows the true purpose. We have faith that God has a plan, and if we can get anyone closer to God with your story, that is enough for me to see the purpose of this tragedy. It is not fair, but it is God's work and we have to accept this new life and be grateful for your life and God's love."

Excerpt from Journal Entry, January 07, 2021

CHAPTER 15

System Failure

I was lost in thought, staring out the window of Charlie's room at the changing landscape below. The leaves, once fiery red and golden yellow, were now beginning to brown. A gust of wind swept across the parking lot, sending a cascade of leaves tumbling to the ground and sailing across the asphalt. Cycling of the seasons was marking time in the most poignant of ways; the changes outside seemed to parallel changes we were experiencing on the inside. At times it felt we were withering, shedding facets of who we used to be. But I held in my heart the knowledge that just as the leaves regenerate, sometimes fuller than before, we too would experience lush growth as pieces of our old life fell away.

Charlie was tired. Her rigorous surgery schedule had her in the OR nearly every day as doctors continued to slough off burned skin and graft the new skin onto her body. Some days,

I'd come to see her and it was as if she hadn't been through anything at all. The morning's surgery seeming like a distant memory. Other days, like today, Charlie's eyes were heavy, her mannerisms betraying her utter exhaustion.

As we sat together, something in the room changed. We were overcome with an unmistakable odor and realized almost immediately where it was coming from. Charlie's fecal management system had failed. The overflow had saturated the bed beneath her, soaking through her gown and pooling on the sheets. Watching Charlie's eyes fill with tears, I ran my hand over her cheek to reassure her, "Honey, I'll be right back. We'll get this taken care of."

She nodded.

I left the room and walked into the hallway looking for someone to help. I finally saw a nurse in the distance and headed in her direction. "Nurse," I started, trying to keep calm, "Charlie's fecal management system has failed and she's sitting in a mess. Can we have someone come in and help get her cleaned up?"

Instead of meeting my level of concern, the nurse simply said, "We'll get someone in as soon as we can."

As soon as we can?

I accepted her answer assuming that someone would be into the room shortly, so I quickly returned to Charlie's side. She lay in her bed with her eyes closed, face scrunched, with tears wetting her cheeks. Her breath was catching as she tried to inhale deeply. I stood by her head and whispered, "I know, honey."

Tears dropped onto her chest.

Minutes went by and soon an hour had passed since I'd seen the nurse in the hallway who had assured me that someone would be in. With every second that slid by, I grew more and more angry with the staff. How could they let someone sit in a mess like this for so long? How could they allow a patient to suffer such indignity?

How?

I kissed Charlie's head and told her I'd be right back. I left the room and jogged to the nurses' station where two nurses were sitting behind the glass chatting.

"What's going on here?" I asked, firmly.

"I'm sorry?" One of the nurses responded.

"I spoke to a nurse one full hour ago about Charlie's fecal management system failing and she's now been sitting in her mess for all that time. Why hasn't anyone come to help us?"

The nurse closest to me leaned forward and said, "I'm sorry, all I can say is that someone will be in soon."

"Soon? What does that mean?" I asked, narrowing my eyes.

"It means we're working on it and will have someone there as soon as we can."

I rubbed my temples and headed back toward Charlie's room not wanting to leave her alone. I couldn't believe what she was being subjected to. There was no excuse for the hospital to leave her sitting in her own feces for hours on end. There was no reason for her to suffer such indignity. And there was nothing I could do ... except show up for my wife.

I walked quickly back into the room where Charlie still sat overcome with emotion. I pulled up my chair next to her wishing I could cradle her in my arms and take the pain away.

"This sucks," she whispered.

"I know, it does," I responded, reaching for her hairline to softly caress her scalp.

After another hour, and another I continued to leave the room periodically to find out what was going on, to shout, to do anything I could to get someone to listen to me. But it all fell on deaf ears. The helplessness I felt was inescapable, threatening to drown me as I watched Charlie suffer. Here I was, a strong, educated entrepreneur, a warrior for my wife, a force to be reckoned with. Yet, I was unable to get anyone to listen. I couldn't make a change. I couldn't get anyone to recognize that my wife was a human being forced to suffer indignities beyond measure.

Exhausted from hitting dead end after dead end, I decided the best thing I could do was to sit with Charlie and allow the despair to overcome us. We let the moment envelop us, and instead of fighting the pain, trying to keep it at bay, we gave the grief space. Together, we wept, casting prayers and wishes into the unknown, resting together in the stark reality of where we were forced to be. Charlie was always strong, rarely letting her situation get the best of her. Yet, here, in this space, I could see cracks forming.

She was going to break.

Our tear-filled eyes met. I got as close to her as I possibly could and said, "Charlie, let's never forget the feeling we are having right now. We are at rock bottom and as horrible as this is, I don't want to forget it. There will be a day when we are back on top, and I want us to be forever grateful because we rose from this experience."

"I know," she mouthed, a gush of tears rushing down her face.

"Honey, we are broken right now. We will take this day to sob and feel all the sorrow for all you've been robbed of, but tomorrow, we will find peace and will refocus on gratitude because you are alive."

Together, we continued to grieve, letting huge, guttural cries escape from time to time. We purged ourselves of anger, fear, and frustration, allowing each feeling to sink into our hearts in hopes it would pass.

It would be more than two hours before anyone came to clean Charlie up and give her back some semblance of dignity. Two hours of mourning. Two hours of suffering. Two hours of wrenching pain. But we made a promise to one another in that seemingly endless stretch of time. Tomorrow, we will be grateful.

The next day I arrived at the hospital to see life back in Charlie's eyes. Color had returned to her cheeks and her mouth was upturned into a smile.

"How are you feeling today?" I asked, kissing her forehead.

"Grateful," she mouthed.

"I love you so much," I responded.

I glanced over Charlie's shoulder, staring back at the falling leaves I'd watched the day before. Branches continued to bow in the breeze, sending leaves twirling to the ground. I took in a deep breath, allowing myself to sink into the gratitude, feeling hopeful about our inevitable rise back from the depths where we found ourselves. This experience was a stark reminder of the power of the mind and the importance of intentionally processing grief, loss, and hopelessness. I was beginning to see my own evolution taking shape as I stopped trying to fight feelings, meeting them with aggression and beating them back with all my strength. I had entered a phase where I could see the loss of control and advocate for Charlie without losing sight of what really mattered: our family's bright future.

CHAPTER 16

Collar

Thanksgiving slid by like an old friend passing through town who never stopped to say, "hello." In the past, the holiday was marked with the most delectable of meals. A golden-brown turkey with succulent gravy, mashed potatoes piled high, green bean casserole, squash casserole, yeast rolls, and perfect pairings of wine. We'd pray, then enjoy our meal, catching up with family, reminiscing about the past and dreaming about the future. We'd then retire to the living room for coffee, gearing up to sample sweet treats, each made with the greatest of care.

This year, Thanksgiving had been like any other day. The boys playing on the floor while we unceremoniously ate food neighbors and friends had brought by. As my mom and I sat and watched the boys, I yearned for them to have their mother here with them. I knew that no matter how hard I tried or how much I pushed to keep things in order, I simply couldn't replace a mother's love.

At the hospital, Charlie was still on and off the ventilator, the size of the collar causing major frustration and excruciating pain. However, we had gone two months without incident, and it was beginning to feel safe to explore the idea of downsizing again. Although I still carried some fear, things felt different now. Charlie had been making strides in her recovery and each surgery went by without incident. The more I thought about it, the more I felt it was time for me to begin gently nudging the staff once more.

This time, things were far simpler. I asked Dr. Bergin and he said that the collar would be downsized in the OR during her next surgery *if* she were able to be off the ventilator for 48 hours without her levels dropping. I was thrilled. With Christmas next on the list, I knew there would be few presents that would bring more relief than a smaller collar, which would come with the ability to speak.

Charlie made it through that 48 hours without any problems and I was excited to get to the hospital that Friday to finally be able to see her in a size six collar—one that actually fit. For the entire early morning as I went about my routine, I smiled thinking about how much progress we had made and how close we were to making huge strides. At 9 a.m. I called the nurse's station for a morning update and to find out what time they planned on downsizing the collar.

"Unfortunately, Mr. Xavier," the nurse chirped, "the doctors in the OR have decided not to downsize the collar today. They'd like to wait another 48 hours with her off the ventilator to see how her levels look."

There it was—the white-hot anger, more intense than I'd felt yet on this journey—rising in my throat.

We'd come so far.

They'd made us a promise.

They were pushing us off.

This gift for Charlie was slipping away.

I could only muster one question: *Why?*

"I'm not sure. I'll have the OR doctor call you shortly," then she hung up.

My mind raced. I was in a full rage spiral. I wanted to hurt someone; to make the doctors pay for making my wife suffer. But then I took a breath and reminded myself that anger would get me nowhere. I simply needed to get to Charlie's side and fight for her like the valiant warrior I'd become.

By 2 p.m. I was in the car and on my way to the hospital. My phone finally rang when I was 30 minutes out and I pressed the button on my car's Bluetooth to answer. On the other end was the ICU doctor who had good news. He let me know that he was incredibly pleased with Charlie's healing and continued to talk about how well she was doing. All the while, I was ready to scream

"Do you have any other questions?" he asked.

"Yes," I said, trying to remain calm. "We were told her collar would be downsized today. Why wasn't it done?"

Sensing my anger, the doctor said it would be best for me to speak directly to the ICU attending doctor.

When I arrived at the hospital, I stormed into the building and up to the burn unit, demanding to see the attending doctor as soon as possible. Of course, the doctor made me wait more than 30 minutes before she entered Charlie's room.

Without properly greeting her I began, "May I ask why you decided that Charlie would not have her trachea collar downsized today?"

She asked me to remind her of Charlie's ventilator status and I replied that she'd been off the ventilator for more than 48 hours and therefore should have been downsized that day.

"Well, if that's the case, she should have been downsized today, but now it's too late in the day to do it. I will be willing to revisit it tomorrow since I will be the attending in the morning."

"But tomorrow is Saturday," I said, narrowing my eyes. "You'll be short staffed."

"Friday night is worse," she replied. "Let's do this. I will personally downsize Charlie at 9:30 tomorrow morning."

I looked her in the eyes and said, "Do I have your word that tomorrow, no matter what, she will be downsized at 9:30 a.m.?"

"Yes," she replied.

We shook hands.

"I don't recall ever negotiating a procedure with a patient or family member," she said with a smile.

"Well," I responded, "I'm not your typical family member."

The next morning, as promised, Charlie was downsized to a size six collar. As soon as I was able to see her after the procedure, which she tolerated perfectly, I wanted to shout with joy. A wide smile had returned to her face, along with the hope that welled inside her. This was the first major stride toward normalcy we had made in these three months, and it felt incredible. I had spent months begging, hours upon hours researching, and expelled more energy than I thought I possessed. With the smaller collar, she would be able to talk, greatly reducing her frustration since she would be able to clearly express in a rasp what she wanted to say, and she would also be able to have liquids and eventually food. She could feel less trapped and less like a patient, and more like a human. I tried not to think about how André *before* might have handled Charlie's complaints of discomfort, and it didn't matter anyway. This gift, the gift of comfort, is one I yearned to give her, and that yearning was born of all the ways I was evolving on this harrowing journey.

"When you know you are right, don't ever stop until you achieve what you need or want if you are right, don't let anyone tell you otherwise!"

—Excerpt From Journal Entry November 30, 2021

CHAPTER 17

Suffering in Silence

No matter how well things went or how many victories we had, fear still lurked around every corner. The one thing that never disappeared was concern over infection since her chance of suffering a serious one was sky high. Miraculously, however, Charlie suffered a total of seven infection scares, and out of those seven, two were truly confirmed. One was an upper respiratory infection due to the use of the ventilator. They called it pneumonia, but it never went to her lungs. It just stayed in her trachea. The second one was a urinary tract infection due to her urinary catheter.

Medical standard of care demands daily blood work for a burn patient, which was one thing about standard of care I could get behind. Each day, a nurse would arrive to take blood through Charlie's port because she didn't have enough skin for a nurse to be able to take it from the vein.

We held our breath every time they sent a blood sample out. I thought I would eventually begin to become desensitized to the pattern, but I never did. Waiting for those results felt like a matter of life and death every single time.

Watch for symptoms.

Take a blood sample.

Send the sample out.

Wait for an agonizing 24 hours to see if the sample grew anything.

If it did, take another blood sample and start broad-spectrum antibiotics.

Wait another 24 hours to see what the culture grew so we would know the specific antibiotic to treat her.

Cross-contamination was always possible at the site of Charlie's port. It was commonplace for infection to occur there simply because it was an open wound. Air and blood both got into that opening, so it was fertile ground for bacteria.

Just like the ventilator, I had hard relationship with antibiotics. If Charlie had a bacterial infection, we needed the antibiotics to kill it as quickly as possible. But if she didn't have an infection, the use of antibiotics was likely to create a resistance to certain good bacteria and could even prevent them from working effectively in the future. The fear of infection and all that came with it was like a ghoul, constantly hovering over us.

One Thursday morning, I walked into Charlie's room and began to rattle off all the things the boys had being doing that day.

"What?" Charlie asked.

I repeated myself.

"What?" she asked once more.

I repeated myself at least three more times, but Charlie inexplicably couldn't hear me. She finally got frustrated and whispered, "Never mind."

What the heck?

Why can't she hear?

What's going on?

The first thing I thought is that Charlie had a wax buildup in her ears. There are a few things the hospital won't do. Cleaning a patient's ears and cutting their nails are two of them. I guess the risk of infection is just too high.

I started begging for the staff to clean her ears. By then the staff knew well enough that I wouldn't stop until Charlie got what she needed.

"Fine, André. We will clean her ears."

The nurse practitioner came in and started cleaning Charlie's ears. "They are actually not too bad," she said, inspecting the tip of the swab. She gently placed a scope in her ear and said, "Yeah, there is very little wax in here, but I do see what looks like fluid behind her ear."

Finally. An easy fix.

I lived for the days when we encountered a problem that they could easily take care of, and I knew that fluid could be drained in mere moments by a specialist.

I immediately asked for an Ear, Nose, and Throat consult.

The answer was a resounding *no.*

"I'm sorry," the nurse responded, "an ENT is only for outpatients."

"What are you talking about? She's in the ICU. Everything is an emergency!" I said, raising my voice. I was getting rattled.

So, I did what I did best—push, push, push.

And I eventually won.

The ENT came the next day and performed a hearing test. He gave no indication of his findings while he was in the room, so once again, we were forced to wait.

When Saturday came and I hadn't heard back about the test results, I gently nudged. I tried not to do everything full force. I was finally told by Charlie's doctor that the ENT delivered the results and reported that there was no fluid behind her ears.

"Great news," I said, trying not to sound sarcastic. "So, why can't she hear?"

"Well, she can't hear because she's sick. She's been on and off the ventilator and that's why."

That wasn't an acceptable explanation.

Later that day, the doctor had to come in and do a procedure to change the arterial line in Charlie's groin area. I got as close as I could to Charlie's ear and whispered loudly, "Honey, here is what is happening. They are saying that there is no fluid behind your ear. I believe there *is* fluid behind your ear because the nurse said there was. They are not willing to have the ENT come and redo the test. A different doctor is coming in a little while to change your arterial line. What if you decline access for them to change your line until you get your hearing test done?"

I knew what her answer would be.

Deal.

When the doctor came in, I relayed the message. "Charlie is not going to let you change her line until we get a hearing test done."

He was stunned. "What?"

Confidently, I said, "As the patient, Charlie can decline care and she is not going to allow the line change unless she can have a second opinion on the hearing test."

He left the room befuddled. I could tell he'd never had a patient refuse any kind of care as a bargaining tactic. But my, did it work. Within the hour, we got a phone call from the doctor who did the initial test.

"This is Dr. So-and-so. I'm the doctor who looked at your wife's ears and there is no fluid behind her ears."

I raised the same question I had earlier. "Then, why can't she hear?"

He gave me the same spiel about Charlie being on and off the ventilator and being very sick, which had led to hearing loss. He said it with confidence and pride—like he had all the answers, and I wasn't privy to how he arrived at them. I didn't care about his confidence. It still didn't make sense to me.

"Well, I believe there is fluid," I replied.

"Why?"

"Because the nurse practitioner looked and said she saw fluid. Charlie can't hear now, and her hearing was perfectly fine just days ago."

The doctor was getting a little more frustrated and retorted, "A *nurse practitioner* is not a doctor. I am a *doctor*. I am an ENT. I know exactly what I'm talking about."

I knew this was one of those situations that could easily escalate, so I made sure to use the lowest tone I could muster when I said, "Okay, but what if you are wrong?"

"I'm not wrong."

I wasn't backing down. "I know you *say* you are not wrong, but what if you are?"

He spat back, "Well, there's nothing that you can do about it because I did the test, and these were my findings."

I immediately asked for a supervisor.

"There is no supervisor, sir. Today is Saturday. I'm the only one here, and you are stuck with me."

Stuck?

No, I am never stuck.

I matched his intensity and raised the stakes it a little. "If it ends up that you were wrong and she does have fluid behind her ears, and then develops an infection and dies, I can sue you."

I will never forget his ridiculous answer as long as I live. "No, you can't, because even if she has fluid behind her ear, that fluid is sterile."

Thanks to my reading of dozens of medical papers on infection, I knew that was absolutely not the case. I'd read several case studies that talked about patients getting bacterial infections from fluid because it can carry bacteria.

My voice raised, I came right back at him, "Are you sure about that? Because I can prove otherwise."

"This conversation has no place here," he said. "You're asking questions that are not applicable to Charlie's case."

By this time, I was yelling on the phone. Just then, Charlie's surgeon, the director of the burn unit, walked by on his rounds and heard me.

"What's going on, André?"

I slammed the phone down on its base and proceeded to tell him the full story. I told him Charlie had refused to have her line replaced until she had the test. Knowing how high the stakes were with her line replacement and possible infection at the site, the surgeon convinced us to allow the line change and promised that he would personally see that she had her second opinion the next day. I hated this tactic, but it worked. Staunch negotiation was proving to get Charlie the care she deserved.

The very next day, Charlie finally got her second opinion, and no surprise to us, she had fluid behind her ears. On her next trip to the OR they inserted tubes to drain the fluid and, immediately, she could hear again.

It is such a vicious cycle. My nemesis, the ventilator, was the culprit. When Charlie was not on the ventilator, breathing on her own, she was equalizing her ears constantly. She was getting the air out. However, in her time on the ventilator, that buildup of pressure continued for a long time, and since she was not breathing through her nose, the moisture from the ventilator started to build up. It had seeped into her ear and caused the infection, which worsened over time. At that point, we found out Charlie suffered a mild high-pitch hearing loss also due to the use of antibiotics. It is a permanent loss.

The same lesson kept coming to me; ask questions and then push when need be. Sometimes push hard. If I hadn't stood up for Charlie and advocated for her rights as a patient, she might be deaf right now. I couldn't help but wonder what happened to patients without advocates, those with advocates who were afraid to speak up, or those whose advocates did not have access to the education I did

When I eventually spoke to the chair of the department about the incident, I pleaded, "Will you make sure that that doctor knows that he was wrong, and that next time it would be a good idea to be humble and accept the possibility that he could be wrong? I want him to know to always ask for a second opinion because he could have cost my wife's hearing."

I was given a nod and a promise of a conversation with the original ENT. I knew this promise was empty, but I was too tired to care.

"It was a mixed feelings visit, in one hand it is almost surreal to be talking about Charlie's rehabilitation, and in the other hand is a new reality that we will need to learn all about it ... I am grateful for the opportunity to have such a world class facility near us, so Charlie can receive the best possible care, but it will be an adjustment, especially since Charlie will be spending a good amount of time in there, we don't know yet how long, but we do know it will be a while."

Excerpt from Journal Entry, December 8, 2021

CHAPTER 18

Sheltering Arms

After I parked, I sat in my car with my eyes closed, letting the bright sunshine warm my face as it streamed through the windshield. Sometimes, I would do this; just linger in the car for a moment in a parking lot, or in my driveway, enjoying a moment of silence. Life was so filled with beeping, whirring machines, pinging phones, and squealing children that the only quiet I experienced was quiet I sought. In this moment, I desperately needed to center myself. This was a big moment. I was about to tour a world-class rehab facility: Sheltering Arms Physical Rehabilitation.

I opened my eyes and let myself focus on the building, which was massive and modern from the outside. It was multi-level, made of metal and glass, and stretched as far as I could see. I drew a breath then stepped out of the car, taking in the unseasonably warm temperatures. I pulled on my mask as I crossed the parking lot and breezed through the front door. I was immediately grateful for the way Sheltering Arms felt. It was inviting, bright and alive with a feeling of hope. There was a brightly lit Christmas tree in the corner and expertly hung garland surrounding each window. The decorations were tasteful and lush, nothing like the haphazard, seemingly forced decorations in hospital hallways.

I made my way to the front desk where an admissions specialist greeted me. "Mr. Xavier," she chirped. "It's fantastic to finally meet you. I've heard so much about Charlie. How is she doing?"

She was so genuine and so warm that I immediately relaxed in her presence. "She's doing really well, thank you."

"Well, we are so excited to begin our work with her," she responded. "Let me show you around."

I followed the admission specialist past the reception area and into the facility, which I learned was just two years old. There was exercise equipment, racks of medicine balls, and a station for assisted stretching. I was struck by how clean and shiny everything was and how engaged every member of the staff seemed. As we walked by, physical therapists might look up and nod, hello, but they were otherwise completely focused on their patient, keeping them on track as they completed their exercises.

As we turned a corner, I peered over my shoulder and could hardly believe my eyes. Walking about 50 feet behind us was a quadriplegic man, strapped to robotic legs and arms, which he was operating with his physical therapist by his side. I stopped and watched as he walked, placing one metal leg in front of the other as he made his way down the hallway. I couldn't believe what I was seeing. It was simply miraculous. As the man walked by, we continued down the hallway to a huge, clean room lined with big, wooden desks. There, occupational therapists were helping patients practice everyday tasks, like brushing their hair, using utensils, and moving small objects from one place to another. The more I saw, the more excited I became to think about Charlie working toward a life of greater independence. I pictured her seated at one of those stations, laughing with her own occupational therapist as she re-learned to perform tasks on her own. Just walking these hallways gave me such a deep feeling of hope. There was *life* after.

Finally, as the tour was wrapping up, I was taken to see where patients lived, each in their own room. I smiled broadly the moment we walked through the door into one of the empty rooms. I could hardly believe the contrast between this room and Charlie's room at the hospital, which was dark and basic. This room was spacious with a neat, comfortable-looking bed in the center. There were dressers with drawers and a big space in front of a mirror where someone could easily dress. With high ceilings and bright, natural light filtering in through big windows, the room felt like it should be occupied by a person—not a patient. The rooms were even outfitted with smart TVs and bathrooms with walk-in showers. I felt tingly with excitement about Charlie getting the chance to live in one of these sleek, beautiful rooms as she worked through the in-patient program—her last stop before coming home to the boys and me.

Following the tour, I was able to sit down and speak with the specific staff members who would be caring for Charlie. Each one was nicer than the last. As I spoke with the team, it became abundantly clear just how unique Charlie was and how hard they were working to create care plans just for her. I was so used to being in the burn unit with Charlie; a place where burn treatment and care of burn victims is an everyday thing. Yet, at the rehab facility, it seemed no one had even met a survivor like Charlie with burns over 85 percent of her body. Sadly, this is because most burn victims do not survive and therefore never make it to rehab. This reality kept in perspective how blessed we were and how supernatural Charlie's recovery really was. This meant she would need an extraordinary team by her side as she continued to heal.

We had found that team.

As I exited the facility, as happy as I was, I couldn't completely give into the joy. A huge part of me was so excited to see Charlie settled into Sheltering Arms institute. I could hardly wait to see her making progress toward each and every goal she had, from small things like getting back into the kitchen to big things, like getting back on her feet. Yet, another part of me felt the pull of sadness. The end of Charlie's stay in the hospital meant the beginning of a whole new journey; one that would test her strength and mental fortitude just as much, if not more. Although I knew this was something Charlie could handle, I couldn't help but hold a moment to grieve for her. My God, were we grateful for our new and exciting lives, but I'd be lying if I told you there was never a time I wished to go back to *before*. As I got into my car, closed the door, and let the silence swaddle me, I dreamed of a time when Charlie no longer had to stare down the great unknown.

"Charlie was so grateful once she heard my list of fears, and my promise to be at her side at each step, she was able to express such gratitude with her eyes and words, it was one of the most beautiful moments since the accident, we are now feeling light..."

—**Excerpt From Journal Entry December 9, 2021**

CHAPTER 19

Drawing Close

Most days, I sat at Charlie's bedside and we would simply fill each other in on the day. After I showed her pictures and videos of the boys, which was a daily occurrence, we'd settle into conversation, which Charlie still managed in whispers despite the trach. I would tell her about my successes and failures, and she would tell me about her breakthroughs and her breakdowns. Typically, following our conversation, we would settle on watching a show or a movie to bring some normalcy to the situation. In the warm glow of Charlie's iPad, we could forget for a few moments here and there that we were stuck in a situation we'd never wish on anyone.

One December day as cold rain beat against the window in Charlie's room, I noticed a shift in her mood. We'd just finished talking about the boys and looking over pictures from the night before when Charlie gave me a look I hadn't seen before. Her cheeks were red, her brows knitted together.

"What's wrong?" I asked, softly.

I was taken aback when she stared into my eyes, her lips quivering, her cheeks wet.

"I feel like an idiot," she whispered.

"What do you mean?" I asked.

Her breath caught as she managed, "I wish I hadn't gone to Patch that day."

"Oh, my love," I responded.

"I wish I had stayed home ..."

She continued, listing off her wishes one by one.

She wished she hadn't sanded the frame that day.

She wished she would have dropped and rolled faster.

She wished she could turn back time.

I moved closer to her and gently touched her face. She continued whispering all her deepest, darkest feelings about that day and how torturous recovery had been and would continue to be. She grieved her life, she'd miss both boys swiftly approaching birthdays, Christmas, and all other momentous occasions to come. She was in excruciating pain all the time and hated relying on whispers and lip reading to express herself. She needed her voice.

I listened. I showed compassion. I felt empathy. I felt deep, helpless pangs of sorrow. And this deep, mournful sorrow was something I hadn't yet shared with Charlie. I'd remained positive around her always, showing her only my love, strength, and resolve. I'd fought for her valiantly, I'd made her feel as comfortable and cared for as possible while hiding negative emotions deep inside. But Charlie's transparency opened space for me to share with her what my real experience had been;my grief, my emotional struggles, my regrets, my fears, my evolution.

I filled the space Charlie had opened with something no one had ever seen from me; I allowed myself to be vulnerable. I shared with her the fear that overwhelmed me when I thought that she was not going to make it, I told her how I felt responsible for the accident, I told her how overwhelming my days could be, how I missed her every moment of the day, but especially at night when we used to hold one another. I told her how hard I worked to be strong, how I pushed myself into battle again and again even though sometimes I felt like I too would collapse under the weight of it all.

Together, Charlie and I wept, finally allowing ourselves to drop our positive attitudes and hopeful outlooks, even for just a moment. Although we couldn't physically wrap ourselves around one another, our hearts became braided together as we mourned the past and grieved the future we'd once been so certain of. Though firmly planted in that moment, each cascading tear gave way to a certain freedom. Finally allowing one another to see emotions we'd hidden away opened the door for a new kind of honesty. From that point forward, Charlie and I agreed that we could visit the dark side from time to time. We could feel safe with one another to go down the rabbit hole and fall apart when we needed to. However, we promised never to linger in the dark for too long. Instead, we'd allow a release of the bad to make room for the good.

"Charlie's story is proof that God still performs miracles, and that Love, kindness and faith can conquer anything!"

Excerpt from Journal Entry, October 11, 2021

CHAPTER 20

Sundays

For our little family, Sunday was always the most special day of the week. We'd wake together and have a small breakfast, then we'd drive to our local parish, Holy Comforter Catholic Church. Although I was born Catholic, Charlie only converted about six years before the accident. Yet, she became an even better Catholic than I was and never let us miss a service. Too young for Confraternity of Christian Doctrine (CCD), the boys would slide into the pews with us, Julien on Charlie's lap, London between us. We'd listen to the sermon, take communion, and spend time in prayer. Then, following church, we would head to the downtown mall for brunch, which was always Charlie's favorite. She loved to order French Toast with a side of bacon and, of course, a mimosa. We'd clink our glasses and talk about the service as the boys colored on their placemats. I loved those days so much; Sunday morning always felt like a pause in a life that never seemed to stop moving.

Since the accident, my relationship with God had changed. I had always been a devout Catholic I knew the power of God's grace and I had faith, but until this experience with Charlie, I'm not sure I really knew what that meant. Yes, I believed in God. Yes, I went to mass. But that's where it ended. Once we stepped back through the doors and went about the ritual of our Sundays the meaning behind God's words, the splendor of His glory, simply fell away. I lived my life the way I wanted. I prioritized success at all costs. I was hard. I was tough. I was cutting. But I honored God when I had time. I thought that was enough.

When the accident happened, my immediate reaction was to feel cynical. My heart was so heavy with fear, it was nearly impossible to see my faith through the clouds. I felt like a rat in a cage, searching for a way out; an exit from the stark reality facing me. Yet, the only thing that felt natural to me at that time was to pray. I spent every moment in prayer—whether it was at the hospital, at home with the boys, in my car, or on the floor crying. I begged God for mercy. I begged him for strength. And He provided.

As time went on, I no longer saw worship as something relegated to Sundays. I spent much of my life in prayer, sometimes with Charlie, sometimes with the boys, and sometimes all alone. He has met every prayer with deep love and affection, constantly keeping His hand on Charlie's back and mine, guiding us through this experience, reminding us that even when all seems lost, there is a purpose, and He will slowly reveal it.

In all this, I began to see Sundays differently. If daily prayer was like filling my tank with regular, unleaded gasoline, Sunday mass was like filling it with jet fuel. Those days became so special to me, allowing me to recharge in ways I never felt I could alone. With the boys at home with my mom, I would sit in the pew, gaining a deeper understanding of His words and what they meant. I found myself nodding, taking notes, locking away every ounce of His glory so I might call on it during the week. It was as if I was now living my faith in technicolor, broadening my relationship with Him, testing the limits to see how deep I could go. No matter what obstacle I have encountered or how hard I was taking things, God never failed to show up.

Of course, there are moments when it feels hard to keep the faith. When I watch Charlie on a rough day with her Rheumatoid Arthritis recovering from a particularly hard surgical procedure, or simply having a bad, sad day, I want to jump in and save her. I want to erase the pain. I want to turn back time. I want to gather all the bad things and banish them. Yet, my faith has reminded me that suffering has a purpose. Pain has a point. We may not yet see it, but we will when He is ready to reveal His plan. That thought alone has kept me strong in some of Charlie's darkest moments and has allowed me to carry on with the deep, unwavering knowledge that one day, His plan will become crystal clear.

"Charlie has become passionate about one day speaking out about Patient Advocacy. She said she wants to make sure every patient has that same level of comfort in knowing their rights are being protected."

—**Excerpt From Journal, January 13, 2021**

CHAPTER 21

Power of Attorney

One snowy morning before my trip to the hospital, I sat scanning my emails. A lightning bolt of stress shot through me as I saw an email from our mortgage company

REMINDER: ACTION NEEDED TO COMPLETE YOUR REFINANCE

I had completely forgotten about our refinance!

I called the mortgage company trying to explain our situation to the representative. When I told him about Charlie's accident and the fact that she was in the hospital undergoing surgery after surgery, they educated me on the importance of a Power of Attorney. My heart fell. I wished I could reach into my filing cabinet and pull out that all important piece of paper, or that I could pull up a scanned copy on my phone in a snap. However, like most people, Charlie and I had never considered tragedy an option, so we didn't have a Power of Attorney. I wish I could have just given up on the refinance, but due to the mounting financial pressure caused by astronomical medical bills, there was no choice. I *had* to complete the refinance, which meant I needed a Power of Attorney as soon as humanly possible.

There was just one thing.

The hospital had a rule that Charlie was only allowed to have one visitor at a time. Yet, for Charlie to sign the Power of Attorney, we needed signatures from two witnesses who personally knew Charlie before the accident. The strict COVID-19 policy also meant neither the attorney nor the notary could be present either.

As always, I leaned on my investigative skills and I learned that in Virginia, you can use what is called a remote notary. In other words, I could be in the room with Charlie and we could be on a video conference with all parties involved. That way, our two witnesses could see Charlie signing the Power of Attorney. After checking with Charlie's friends to see when they could make the trek to the hospital, I let the nurses know that we would be coming on Sunday to sign the papers so they would know what to expect.

I called my case manager and the social worker, and said, "Charlie and I have to sign papers to refinance our house that we live in, but to do that, I need to get Charlie to sign a Power of Attorney first."

Their first answer was, "No, she cannot sign anything like that."

I assumed they just didn't understand our dilemma. "Look, I know she can legally sign a Power of Attorney. This is for our house, not anything medical. I just want to give you a heads up I will be coming on Sunday because we need two witnesses to sign who knew Charlie before the accident."

I explained that I would not be breaking any rules regarding COVID-19 protections because I would be the one going into Charlie's room with an iPad doing the video, while the witnesses were downstairs, so they would be on site but would not be coming into Charlie's room. When I hung up, the case manager did not say that I was not allowed to do it, she left me with the impression that I could do as I explained.

That Sunday, Charlie's friends drove all the way from Charlottesville to Richmond. They met with the notary in the lobby of the hospital, and I set off upstairs with the iPad.

When I got to the burn unit, the nurse was not at the desk, so I went on into Charlie's room. The notary called on the telephone and started asking Charlie her qualifying questions.

What is your name?

What is the year?

Who is the President?

Do you know what kind of document you are signing?

And what is today's date?

The State of Virginia says if you can answer those five questions, you are capable of signing a legal document. Charlie was nailing each question one by one.

In the middle of the last question, a nurse stormed into the room and bellowed, "You have got to stop what you are doing. You cannot video chat in here!"

Another nurse yelled from the back, "Security is on their way up! You have got to stop!"

Charlie looked at me with a puzzled look, and I just wanted to keep her from getting upset. I smiled at her and added, "Let me turn off this call and let me see what's going on."

I stepped outside of Charlie's room and the nurse said, "Sir, you are not allowed to do that."

That's when security arrived—a team of two huge guys who escorted me out of the unit and led me to the conference room. I asked to speak to the person in charge.

Within moments, the clinical administrator walked in and demanded to know what was going on. I calmly explained that I was having my wife sign a Power of Attorney so that I could sign our refinance closing papers.

"Mr. Xavier, you are being incredibly deceptive trying to sneak in here on a Sunday to get this done under the radar!"

Under the radar?

I felt so betrayed. These people knew me. I had come there every single day for three months straight, never missing even one day. They knew what we had been through. They knew how our entire family had suffered as a result. And now they were accusing me of trying to coerce my wife into signing papers? For what? Did they think I would try to do *anything* to harm my wife?

I grew furious and requested the names and titles of everyone involved and said I would be back Monday after I had spoken with my attorney.

When I went back into the room, Charlie was confused. From her perspective, the nurse was just doing her job and the whole ordeal was awkward and embarrassing.

I spoke to my lawyer the following day and his advice was, "Look, you are right. They don't have a legal right to prevent Charlie from signing a Power of Attorney. But you will attract more bees with honey than vinegar. Go back there tomorrow and talk with them. No threat of a lawsuit."

I just wanted to know that, should I have a problem, we could sue them for violating our rights.

"Yes, you can, Andre, but trust me, it's not the route we want to go."

The next day, when I got to the hospital, I went to the social worker and asked again. I told her the whole story, and she immediately answered, "I'm sorry. That's not going to happen."

"Why? I just don't understand."

"Charlie is not capable of signing a legal document."

Again, things weren't making sense to me. "Why is she not capable? She does not have a brain injury. She's not in a coma. She's not crazy."

Dr. Bergin who is also the director of the unit had six other people with him when he showed up to Charlie's room and asked me to come with them. We all filed down the hallway into the conference room to hash this out.

I plead my case *again*. "I need to sign this document to refinance our house."

Dr. Bergin insisted that Charlie was not able to sign the Power of Attorney.

"Says who?"

"Says me."

"Look, Doc," I responded, "no disrespect to you, but in the State of Virginia, the only person who can deem someone incapacitated and unable to sign a Power of Attorney is a judge. Legally, you cannot."

The room was silent.

Finally, he responded, "Okay, André, let me talk to some people and see what I can do for you."

Another hour went by, and Dr. Bergin came back to me with a new idea that he and the team assumed I would blindly accept. "We're going to need to send Psychiatry to evaluate Charlie to see if she is capable of signing a legal document."

I didn't love the idea because it seemed risky. If this psychiatrist somehow deemed Charlie incapacitated, the hospital could try to claim guardianship of her in some way. There was no way I wanted to let that happen, but this was Charlie and I had to trust her. Her body had been burned. She had not suffered a brain injury. There was no way a psychiatrist would deem her incapacitated. I took a deep breath and gave in.

Another 20-minutes went by, and an older woman walked into the room and introduced herself as the psychiatrist then continued, "I was asked to complete an evaluation on Charlie. May I ask you to step outside so I can talk to your wife?"

"Sure," I said, "But before I go, I just want to make sure that you see the document that I'm trying to get Charlie to sign." I showed her the Power of Attorney for the refinance.

"Wait a second, this is a legal document. I was asked to do a medical consent evaluation."

I calmly said, "No, they were not honest with you. That's absolutely not true."

She left the room.

Quickly, Dr. Bergin came back into the room and said, "Okay, Andre, you were right. We are going to open an exception one time to you—you may go ahead and have Charlie sign this document."

I was obsessed with the illegality of the situation at this point and semantics threw me into a rage. "No, you are not *allowing* an exception, you're being forced to follow the law—your policy is completely illegal!"

It was several more hours before we were able to get things squared away and the Power of Attorney signed so we could feel a little financial relief, but I still felt rage over the hospital's unjust policy.

I continued to fight for her to be able to sign the legal document for the next week , advocating for everyone who would come after us in this hospital. I had meeting after meeting with person after person, always getting the same run-around story about how they weren't going to change their policy. I finally walked out of one of the meetings and never spoke with anyone about it again. I realized that I was wasting energy in an area that I couldn't control and what I needed to be focusing on was Charlie and the things that I *could* control regarding her recovery.

"It is nice to see the media interested in Charlie's story, but also in this group, the incredible love and support given to us is just unbelievable, and I thank you for being part of this movement, a movement of love and kindness. It gives me hope to see the first glimpse of light coming out of our darkness. I am very hopeful that Charlie's story is touching a lot of people's hearts."

Excerpt From Journal Entry, September 24, 2021

CHAPTER 22

Momentum

It's funny how sometimes something you do that once seemed so small can snowball into something bigger than you'd ever dreamed. When I first started the Facebook journal, it was purely functional. I took the advice of a friend who had been through something similar and decided to speak to everyone all at once about Charlie's recovery, her progress, and how our family was healing. However, what started as a small group of family members soon became a group of 300 loyal followers. That turned into 1,500 followers, then 3,000, and the group just kept growing. A non-native English speaker, I had once been timid about my writing, worried that I'd make mistakes or that my words would lack meaning. However, the more I wrote, the more comfortable I became. After all, I was now a part of something so, so much bigger than I'd ever dreamed.

During this time, I would find myself forgetting how isolated I was, simply because I was too busy to really feel the isolation. I was waking up at the crack of dawn every day to care for Julien and London, getting them ready for the day. Once breakfast was over, they were dressed and ready, my mom would step in, and I would go to my office and attempt to get some work done. Then, I would get into the car and spend two hours driving to Charlie, would spend every moment possible with her, then I would drive the two hours home, arriving just in time for dinner and bedtime with the boys. Once the house was quiet, I would sit down and work on my journal for the day. Those moments in my office in the glow of my desk's little lamp, I would let it all pour out. I'd share as much as I comfortably could without ever exposing too many personal details of Charlie's medical care. The members of the community were so engaging, always posting the most thoughtful, humbling responses to my posts, often sharing their own stories. Having spent most of my life reserved and quiet about my emotions, rarely sharing anything personal with anyone, I realized I was changing. I was willingly opening myself up to the love and support of others and I was grateful to feel less alone. It became my therapy.

Spending time journaling became like spending time with thousands of close friends. They were a group of prayer warriors, support givers, and people who loved harder than I knew was possible. Right from the start, the community didn't just show up online, they showed up in the real world, in real time. If I mentioned that Charlie needed support in the form of cards, thousands of cards would arrive in the mail over the course of a few days. If I said that Charlie loved flowers, she'd receive enough flowers to fill her room with joy. And on the days when Charlie was heading into surgery—which was almost every day—I knew the prayers of love and support would flood in. I firmly believe that those prayers changed the course of Charlie's life, helping her beat the odds again, and again, and again.

As the journal gained momentum, so did interest in Charlie's story. It wasn't long before I was beginning to hear from news outlets about potential local news coverage.

The first contact I received was from a reporter named Rachel Hirschheimer with NBC 29 in Charlottesville who wanted to do a story about the accident. I was comfortable on camera because all the press I had done for my businesses, so I had no worries about my ability to communicate our situation. However, I struggled for a moment because there was no way for me to ask Charlie how she felt about the coverage. However, I rationalized, the Facebook page was live, and the GoFundMe page was fully active and public at that time, so it made sense for me to do the interview in hopes of drumming up more support for fundraising efforts and prayer requests. I'd never hide it from Charlie, but I also wouldn't stress her out by hammering her with questions. So, I decided to set boundaries about what interviews I would conduct and how. Just like in the journals, I vowed to never speak on Charlie's behalf and to never speak about anything that could even possibly paint her in a negative light. I would keep all interviews from my perspective, leaving every ounce of room for Charlie to tell her complete story later. My role was to be a spouse, an advocate.

The first interview I did with Rachel was wonderful. Her reporting was thorough, and she never pushed me to answer any questions that edged too far into Charlie's personal story. We kept things high level and I was able to get the point across that we were still accepting donations through the GoFundMe page and wanted to continue to grow the online community so that we had as many prayer-warriors on our side as possible. Once the interview with Rachel went live, more and more local media picked up the story. I did interviews for print, podcasts, and websites. Each one was about how inspiring Charlie's story was and the fact that we still needed as much support as we could get. Each and every piece was well-received, and the Facebook group kept growing, and growing, and growing.

Then it came: a request from a national outlet asking to cover Charlie's story. They wanted an exclusive, meaning no other news outlet would cover the story. At least not right away.

That was the moment I knew I needed to speak to Charlie more seriously about what was going on with her story and that there was a possibility we could go national. She needed to be a *big* part of this decision since it could have a major impact on our lives.

On that day, I arrived at the hospital to find Charlie in good spirits. She was watching a show on her iPad after her air drying—a process where they allow her skin to dry while exposed. We sat together, looked at my pictures of the boys from that morning, and talked about our days. Finally, I said, "My love, I have to tell you something. You know that I've been doing a lot of local media to bring attention to your story, but I was recently contacted by someone at a national news outlet. And they want an exclusive."

"What does that mean?" she asked.

"Well, it means they want to be guaranteed that they will get the first interview with you when you leave the hospital and head to rehab, then another when you get home. But, again, it's national. This won't be the same as me doing these smaller shows here in town. It won't be contained to people recognizing us at the grocery store and around town when you come home. It'll be bigger. Much bigger."

She stopped to think.

I rubbed her hand.

"It's a big decision, Charlie. This could change your life in more ways than you even realize now. You may lose some of your privacy."

"I know," she said, biting her bottom lip. "The thing is, it's worth it."

"What do you mean?" I asked.

"It's worth losing just about anything to get my story out there. I mean, if it touches one person, one burn victim, and inspires them to keep fighting when they feel like they want to give up, then it's worth it."

I nodded.

She smiled, then repeated, "It's worth it."

"Charlie is in such a good place today! I pray that she continues to heal and get better, God is showing through Charlie that the impossible can be achieved when we have faith! Thank you, God!"

—Excerpt From Journal Entry, December 13, 2021

CHAPTER 23

Brown Paper Packages

Having been through Thanksgiving without Charlie, I had a good idea of what to expect at Christmas. I knew there would be moments at home when I was numb, and some when tears would flow uncontrollably. I'd do my best to keep the holiday spirit alive, but I'd be unable to help coming up short. There was something hollow about the season now—a gaping hole where Charlie belonged. Our house was typically one of the most festive, best-decorated houses in the neighborhood. We'd have glowing lights outside, painstakingly strung, and a gorgeous, full wreath on the door. Inside, every corner of the house would be perfectly staged with trinkets and signs of merriment, so it would be nearly impossible not to become enveloped in the Christmas spirit. We typically had three Christmas trees in the house and about a dozen wreaths handmade by Charlie. From beginning to end, she made the season so glorious, every moment felt like a sip of hot chocolate with a candy cane garnish. Of course, all of Charlie's hard work was in spite of me. "You're such a Grinch," she'd say. Yet, this year, I had to attempt to fill a sliver of her role. I tried my best to decorate; to avoid feeling the full brunt of Charlie's absence, but the effort was futile. Christmas was the time when Charlie was always able to bring magic. Now she remained in the hospital, and I was left to make magic alone.

One of the first things on our list was always to take the boys to have their pictures taken with Santa. This year, I'd take them to a festival for photos, compliments of our friends at Indian Summer Guide Services. We arrived at the event, the boys in outfits Charlie had picked out herself. I fumbled with the car seats, getting both boys out and ready to have fun. Immediately, we were hit with the beautiful joy of the season. There were stations where kids could decorate cookies, pet horses, get creative with arts and crafts, and, of course, meet Santa. The event was a welcome respite from our everyday routine, allowing us to fold ourselves into sweet smells of steaming fried dough, cinnamon cookies, and salty popcorn. The kids were thrilled with every aspect of the event, but as we waited in line to meet Santa, I wondered whether Julien would cry on his lap. I pictured Charlie in this situation, imagining her preparing him to be let go of for a moment, getting excited about meeting a man full of magic. I pictured her putting him down on Santa's lap, then running behind the camera to jump and wave, doing everything she could to get both boys to smile. I hoped I could meet the challenge and get the boys to cooperate, but I had doubts that I'd be able to. As we crept closer, I did my best to pump the boys up with one thing in mind: getting a photo of them smiling with Santa that I could bring to Charlie.

I held my breath as we approached.

Ho, ho, ho!

London scrambled onto one of Santa's knees, then I placed Julien on the other.

I stepped back slowly, ready to jump up and down to keep Julien's cries at bay.

Imagine my shock when I looked back at Julien and his mouth was turned up in a wide smile. He looked at Santa, then back at me, then at the camera, beaming.

Click. Click. Click.

The moment was picture perfect.

And, of course, like everything else without Charlie there, bittersweet.

The next day when I arrived at the hospital, the first thing Charlie asked about was Julien and whether he cried on Santa's lap. I was thrilled to tell her all about the festival and how well the boys did, especially when it was time for them to meet The big guy himself. Charlie sat in her recliner with the biggest smile on her face as she looked at the picture of the boys in their sweet outfits, simply thrilled to be with Santa.

As we talked—Charlie's voice in her usual raspy whisper—something miraculous happened. As she spoke, asking questions and talking about gifts we'd get the kids, her voice began to break through just as she said my name: André. Even without a speaking valve, the smaller trachea collar size had allowed air to get into her vocal cords, thus allowing her to begin to speak.

It had been so long since I had heard the beautiful sound of my wife's voice that I could hardly believe my ears. Charlie and I both burst into tears, trying to grasp the miracle that was unfolding. We continued our conversation about Christmas, Charlie's voice still mostly in a whisper, but some words coming through clearly. That voice—that beautiful voice—was returning.

As Charlie tired, we watched some TV, then she was placed back in her bed. She stared at me, dreamy-eyed and asked what we might get the doctors and nurses as parting gifts when she was discharged to rehab. Charlie was still speaking in a whisper, but as her nurse entered, her voice came through again—this time, I wasn't the only witness.

"Charlie!" Her nurse exclaimed, "I can't believe it. I just heard your voice!"

Charlie's face brimmed with excitement and pride.

The nurse rushed to Charlie's side, "You realize that just three months ago, we weren't sure you were going to make it? And now you're speaking!"

I sat in my corner chair and watched as such raw emotion was exchanged. Her voice continuing to break through, Charlie explained to the nurse just how much she remembered, even from early on. She described her first day at the hospital, how she was brought into a washroom with 20 doctors, nurses, and surgeons there with her. The nurse could hardly believe she remembered so much of that uncertain, harrowing time. She said that most people don't remember their first week in the hospital, let alone their first day.

I could hardly contain my own emotions as I watched as these two women who had been working on Charlie's recovery hand-in hand met a milestone that once seemed so far off. The joy on the nurse's face and the love in her heart were palpable, which caused raw emotion to bubble to the surface for me. I watched as team member after team member came into the room to visit with Charlie, express their love, and tell her how inspiring she was. In that moment, the effect Charlie was having on her team became crystal clear. They weren't just acting as caretakers. They were caring for Charlie like she was a part of their own family. I was beginning to see an even greater softening from the staff that showed me what a positive impact Charlie was having on her medical team. On this journey, she would touch countless lives, but seeing it firsthand was enough to overwhelm me with joy.

Because of Charlie's voice breaking through, she would have her voice valve installed and her first consultation with her speech therapist. Then, she would receive the greatest gift she could possibly hope for: drink training. After all, the unquenchable thirst that I was never able to relieve for her remained. It was a constant, torturous reminder of all she'd endured.

The very next day as I drove to the hospital, my phone rang. To my utter shock, Charlie was on the other end, speaking clearly and distinctly. I could hardly believe my ears—her voice that had been a rasp peppered with the comforting sounds of her voice here and there was now full.

"André!" she exclaimed, "You won't believe it! I can drink liquids again AND guess what? I'm even going to be able to start eating a few foods again soon."

"Oh, honey, that's the best news!" I cried. "What do you want me to bring you?"

Without hesitation, she exclaimed, "Sweet tea from Popeyes!"

"I'm going to get it for you right now. I love you. I can't wait to see you!"

I quickly changed my GPS to navigate me to the closest Popeyes. I pulled up to the window and excitedly ordered a large sweet tea, a large Dr. Pepper, and a full gallon of sweet tea so she had a good supply.

When I arrived at the hospital, I could hardly wait to get to Charlie's room, balancing all the drinks as I went. I ran to the dressing station and quickly performed my routine of scrubbing my hands clean and getting suited up. It was mere moments before

I was entering her room, which had four people inside, the physical therapy team and two nurses. They were all sitting around having the best time talking with Charlie. No one could believe that she was speaking so quickly after having the speaking valve put in. On average, they said it took a few days for patients to begin comfortably speaking with the valve. It took Charlie less than 20 minutes to speak without any trouble breathing.

At first, the pathologist told Charlie that he would return within the next day or two with a machine to run her swallow test, but she wouldn't accept that as an answer. Charlie told the pathologist that he would return that day because she'd been waiting so long for this moment. She explained that she'd been working toward this goal for weeks and wanted nothing more than to complete the test so she could quench the thirst that plagued her first months of recovery.

"Please," she begged, "I've waited long enough."

Within 20 minutes, the pathologist had the machine set up in Charlie's room and was ready to perform the test. She was tested on swallowing liquids, then soft foods, and crackers. She passed the test with flying colors, was cleared to eat a small amount of approved food and drink as much as she wanted.

As soon as Charlie locked eyes on me, her eyes widened. She could see the drink container at my side and began weeping with joy. She had reached a milestone that typically takes weeks for patients to achieve, yet she managed to defy the odds and get there in record time.

Charlie sat in her recliner facing the window, the sun warming her face. As the staff watched, I placed a long straw through the lid and walked toward Charlie with the sweating Styrofoam cup of sweet tea. I settled next to her chair, leaned over and placed the straw at her lips, watching as she took a long, slow sip with her eyes closed. I could see it all—the look of ecstasy as the taste of her childhood swirled in her mouth and cascaded down her throat.

This indescribable moment—a gift undeniably given by *Him*— was proof of God's commitment to Charlie and her miraculous healing.

… we both agreed that our present is where we need to be in right now and enjoy these moments of happiness and gratitude, because we know the future is unsure and it does cause us anxiety, we also agree that looking back at the accident will not bring us any positive feelings, so we are committed to stay in the present and yet be hopeful about the future.

—Excerpt From Journal Entry; December 15, 2021

CHAPTER 24

Blessing

One day early on, I received an unexpected text from a neighbor saying, "Hey, Andre, I wanted to reach out and ask you if it would be okay for me to give your number to a pastor. He is a friend of a friend who wants to make a donation to your family, but it is a considerable gift and they do not want to go through GoFundMe."

"Sure," I responded. "Absolutely! Give him my information. I really appreciate it."

A few weeks went by, and I didn't hear anything from the potential donor, so I texted my neighbor back and she quickly followed up with them.

I got a call two hours later and the gentleman on the other end said, "Hey, André. I am a pastor with a church right outside of Maryland and I run a nonprofit. We have a family who has been touched by your story and they want to make a donation to your family. If possible, I would like to schedule some time so that I can come by your house and meet you."

It turned out, the man I was speaking with was a former police officer turned pastor. He worked mostly with underprivileged families who needed help and could not find it anywhere else. Although his church donated directly to families, in our case, he was approached by a private donor he had never met before. The pastor clarified that since this family was offering the largest gift that the pastor had had the opportunity to give, he wanted to make sure to get to know us before he facilitated the process.

Initially, I hesitated. Although we were *really* financially struggling following the accident, our lives still had the appearance of wealth and comfort. We had nice cars in the driveway and a large home with plenty of nice things inside. I figured the pastor would take one look at our home, turn around, and never come back despite our desperate need. Yet, each time that thought crossed my mind, I kept telling myself that this was old Andre popping up. I no longer identified with the part of myself that assumed the worst of people, believing they were cold and calculating, always suspicious of people's intentions. As these feelings bubbled, I did my best to suppress them, reminding myself of all the good we'd seen since the accident occurred. After all, my family and I had received more kindness than I ever could have imagined. Why should this be an exception?

Not long after our initial call, the pastor arrived at the house to meet the boys and me. After a quick tour, the pastor sat down with me on the couch. We settled quickly into deep conversation about the accident, Charlie's miraculous recovery, and the insanity of our lives at the moment. I found myself crying on and off during our conversation that seemed to last for hours. We prayed together, asking God to continue to heal Charlie and to protect and provide for our family. When we said our goodbyes, I still felt nagging worry that I'd never see or hear from the pastor again.

Yet, the next week, he called.

And the week after that.

And the week after that.

And the week after that.

Soon, I was able to call the pastor my friend.

In the days leading up to Christmas, I had pushed the pastor's offer of a donation so far from my head it was now a distant memory. I was so caught up in preparing for Christmas, keeping things on track with our businesses, caring for the boys, and, of course, visiting Charlie every day, that I had to stay in the moment to survive.

Then, one wintery afternoon, the pastor called. He cheerfully asked if he could come to the house one day soon with two members of his team and take some pictures and a video. Of course, I agreed, and welcomed him and the two girls who came with him into our home.

As we walked through the house, I was keenly aware of my lackluster Christmas decorations and the boys' toys scattered about the floor. The pastor smiled, ignoring everything around us, focusing only on me. As we sat, one of the girls began to film on her phone. The other watched, snapping photos now and again.

In the glow of our modest Christmas tree, the pastor handed me a tiny green gift bag and said, "Open it up."

His smile was warm.

I dug into the bag and found several gift cards inside. He explained these would help with gas and snacks for my two-hour long trips to and from the hospital. A smile spread across my face to meet his. I was so grateful for the gift as the trips back and forth had been so taxing—the relief was so welcome.

"Thank you so much. This is so generous of you; I appreciate it more than you know."

"You're so welcome, André," the pastor said, then added, "There's more."

I dug my hand deeper into the bag until it grazed a folded piece of paper. The girls were still filming and snapping photos as I pulled out what turned out to be a check. When I opened it, my heart stopped. It was more money than I could ever have imagined. My breath hastened—I looked at the pastor, back to the check, to the girls, and back to the check again.

My hands were trembling.

The joy that emanated from within me was unlike anything I had ever experienced before. It exploded from every ounce of my soul, filling the room with radiant joy. I could barely speak, just held my head in my hands and began to weep.

The pastor came over to me and we began to pray together. I could hardly believe what was happening. As a devout Catholic, I have attended church every Sunday since I can remember. Sadly, our parish priest had not been to see us since the accident; he was too busy. Yet, here was this Christian pastor—a man who didn't know me—offering my family something incredible with no expectations or strings attached. There was no agenda, nothing he wanted in return, he just wanted to bless our family.

That Christmas, among all the wonderful gifts I'd received, the priest affirmed something I'd never again allow myself to lose: my faith in humanity.

I was thinking today as I drove back from Richmond, how on this new life, I have learned to really appreciate and take full advantage of every moment, this is how we create memories, this is how we can learn or teach lessons, when we are able to really be present and appreciate each moment in our day, it is almost as if time slows down.

Excerpt from Journal Entry, December 23, 2021

CHAPTER 25

Bittersweet

Although we were deeply committed to living in gratitude, the arrival of Christmas came with a sadness that was palpable. After putting the boys to bed the night before, I'd carefully placed presents under the tree before biting into the cookies and sipping the milk that London was so excited to leave out for Santa. In the dark, the lights from the tree casting shadows on the walls, loneliness overwhelmed me. I steeled myself against the creeping feeling, deciding to focus on the miracles we were experiencing, but I couldn't keep the sadness at bay. My wife was lying in a hospital bed two-hours away and I was playing the part of Santa alone. My heart ached to see Charlie's blond hair glistening in the light as she carefully arranged presents and stuffed stockings just so. I yearned for the sound of paper being trimmed and carefully wrapped around last-minute gifts and the sight of them all; a visible sign of Charlie's beautiful, giving soul, glistening beneath the tree.

I wished to go to bed tangled in her embrace, anticipating the joyous celebration to come. Yet, on that night, I slid into our cold bed alone and pulled the covers over my body tightly, trying to evade the feeling of isolation that threatened to overcome me.

I woke the next morning to the sound of London shouting with joy having run into the living room and seen all his gifts. Julien was making small noises in his crib, so I lifted myself out of bed and went to get him up. I took him into the living room and said excitedly, "Look, Julien, Santa came!"

His eyes lit up as I placed him on the floor and watched him amble toward his gifts.

"Hold on one second, boys," I called out. "Let me call Mommy so she can watch you open your presents!"

I pulled my phone from my pocket and made a FaceTime call to Charlie. She answered right away, "Hi, boys! Did Santa come?" her voice was strained.

I could tell she was holding back tears.

I sat on the floor and tried to hold the camera steady as the boys tore into their gifts, stopping to play with each toy. As hard as I was trying to involve Charlie, I knew it was emotional for her to be missing these precious moments. It was also difficult to get the boys to interact with Charlie on the phone since they were so excited and animated. We stayed on as long as we could, then said goodbye. My heart broke for Charlie, trapped inside the glass box where she'd lived for three months.

After the presents were opened, the paper was cleared away, and the boys were worn out, I set the table. This was typically one of Charlie's favorite things to do—to prepare us for a huge meal she made from scratch. She'd decorate the table with Christmas dishes, candles, and a centerpiece she'd made for the day. I tried not to get lost in memories as I placed our day-to-day dishes on the table paired with everyday silverware and drinking glasses. This year, we were lucky to have received a traditional Ukrainian meal from a family in our community. I'd heated it all on the stove, then called my mom and the boys to gather for the meal. Together, we dug into the cabbage soup, fried fish, and borshch. The boys picked at their food and I tried to enjoy every bite, but it was hard. Although we were so thankful to have food cooked for us, it felt odd to be trying new foods on a day that was typically so special in the most familiar ways.

After we ate, the boys went off and played with their toys while I cleaned up the remnants of a Christmas that felt like it never happened at all.

Later that day I went to see Charlie. I felt an immediate cloud come over me as I approached her room, seeing the sad decorations on the glass. I walked in and tried to remain strong as I kissed her head and told her about the day. Then, we sat together, and I helped her eat a hospital holiday dinner: turkey with mashed potatoes and gravy. The food was bland and flat. It was a steady reminder that we were not home enjoying Charlie's magical cooking. We talked about how much we missed the flavors of the food she made. It's funny how the thought of food can make you homesick for moments, like that first bite of sweet potatoes swirled with allspice, savory meats, or buttery biscuits sopping up all the flavors at once. This Christmas was much like the food on Charlie's plate. A reminder of what once was.

Charlie looked at me from over her plate, her eyes tired, her brows knitted together. "I hate this so much."

"I know," I responded, "It sucks. It really does."

"I want to be grateful, but I can't right now. I miss the boys. I miss being home with you. I miss how Christmas used to feel."

I took a breath, "Charlie, it sucks now, but we have to focus on how incredible it will be when you're home. Next year …"

"I know. I do. But I'm not there yet. All I can think about is how hard it is to be here without you. I'm missing so much."

I reached out and caressed her head, running my fingers along her hairline. She rested her head on her pillow and closed her eyes.

Her wishes filled the room.

"I know that this year will be an amazing one for the simple fact that Charlie will be home this year! I can't express how much I am looking forward for that very special day, but I also know that we still have a long journey before that day, once Charlie is able to leave the hospital, she has to go to rehabilitation and we don't know yet how long she will be there, but I know that each phase that we pass, is one step closer to coming home."

Excerpt From Journal Entry, January 1, 2022

CHAPTER 26

A New Year

We were now officially into the new year and if we squinted, it was almost possible to see the finish line. Charlie's doctor was becoming more and more confident that she should be home for her birthday in June. There are no words to express how thrilled we were to hear this news. Yet, any news during the recovery process is layered and complicated. We knew we still had a long road ahead. Charlie would have to endure many, many more surgeries, more grafting, and would continue to wrestle with the risk of infection for a long time to come. However, even knowing all this, we were able to maintain our positivity.

On that day—the first day of 2022—Charlie and I sat together in front of her window, which was fogged around the edges. We looked out over the trees and the grass, my hand on hers. Charlie sipped her sweet tea. I looked over at her—my beautiful wife. My mind wandered; thing about first dates and stolen kisses. Our hands intertwined. I pictured her big, sparkling eyes on our wedding day as we said "I do" in front of the priest and all of our friends and family. I thought about the two moments when our boys were born and placed on her chest for the first time. I took a breath. I closed my eyes.

I almost lost her.

But I didn't.

The accident happened, yes, but what happened after has revealed to me more beauty than I ever knew existed in the world. My cynicism dropped away, day by day, as Charlie and I experienced the counterpoint of tragedy: love. There were the friends and family members who showed up for us at every twist and turn. There was the online community who offered constant, unwavering support. There was the hospital staff who took such beautiful care of Charlie, she felt loved and protected even when I couldn't be there. And, of course, there was God. When we thought all was lost, He showed us that great loss makes room for exponential gain.

"I am so grateful for God's miracles," I whispered as I stood and kissed Charlie on the head. "You are a miracle."

"I'm so grateful for you and how things with us have changed. I love you so much," she responded, looking up at me.

I stared back.

Tears gathered in the corners of my eyes.

I almost lost her.

But I didn't.

My visit with Charlie was a very good one! She is very excited to share the good news we received today! She may be transferred to a non-ICU room as soon as tomorrow! . . . Things are moving fast and in the right direction, we are beyond grateful!

Excerpt from Journal, February 19, 2022

CHAPTER 27

Touch

Although it had only been months, it felt like Charlie had been living in the ICU for years. In fact, we'd become used to interacting with one another in this new and unusual way, carrying out conversations in what felt like an enclosure at the zoo. Everything in the room had a function and had to be monitored around the clock, so there was constant traffic and no privacy. We'd dim the lights and set up Charlie's iPad on the tray over her bed and would watch movies or TV shows, trying to tune out the sounds of people coming and going. Or, sometimes we'd find ourselves deep in private conversation, needing to pause every few moments to avoid being overheard. It was hard not to feel like our every interaction was supervised. It felt like we were living on display ... because we were.

In addition to the prying eyes, there we barriers, on top of barriers, on top of barriers. I was still wearing full protective gear in her room. That meant gown, shoe covers, gloves, a head cover, a thick N-95 mask, and gloves. My flesh had not touched Charlie's directly since the accident. I did my best to foster our connection, of course. I clumsily ran my gloved fingers over Charlie's scalp. I touched my masked lips to hers. As great as all that was, however, we both yearned for more.

Yet, things were beginning to change. Charlie had progressed so far that her risk level was beginning to drop. She had been off the ventilator for weeks, her stoma opening in her throat for the ventilator tube had healed in record time, and she had passed every test she needed to with flying colors. Thanks to all this, she would be moved out of the burn unit and into a regular, non-ICU room. Other than the N-95 mask I'd still need to wear for COVID-19 protection, I'd no longer need to wear any protective gear when I was with Charlie. This new room would have a bathroom, a shower, and best of all, a door that would no longer remain open at all times.

When I arrived at the hospital on the morning of Charlie's move, it felt strange not to walk into the ICU. Instead, I stopped at the last room in the hallway right before the ICU area was reached. I stood outside the door for a moment, staring at the flowers I had brought with me. My stomach was filled with butterflies. It felt like I was about to greet Charlie for the very first time.

"Knock, knock," I said as I crept inside.

"Hi, babe!" Charlie called. "Look at you—I can see your clothes!"

"I know," I said, spinning with a laugh. "You don't miss the gown?"

"Absolutely not," she said, "Oh my gosh, those flowers are beautiful, thank you!"

"Man, Charlie, I can't believe this. . ."

I looked around the room in awe. There were no monitors beeping or whirring machines. There was only Charlie in her bed, her refrigerator in the corner, and a pile of her things on the windowsill. The silence in the room was one of the most incredible things I have ever experienced. After being surrounded by so much noise for so long, this felt like heaven. As I took it all in, I crossed the room and took my place at her side. I put the flowers on the table in front of her, reached up, and ran my fingernails along her hairline.

She smiled.

I smiled behind my mask.

I reached out my hand.

She smiled wider.

I knelt next to her bed and carefully put my hand on hers. My fingers caressed each groove and gently traced each line. Tears slid down our cheeks as we stared down at our hands, slowly dancing with one another. My heart was soft, my head was full of dreams of the future. My entire being was filled with gratitude.

For a moment as we sat, hand-in-hand, I thought back to how I used to be. I let myself think about the arguments we'd had over silly things I just wouldn't let go. I thought about times when I was harsh with Charlie and hard on our children. I thought about what love meant to me then. If given the chance, I'm not sure I ever would have taken the time to sit next to Charlie, trace her hand, and enjoy the sensations. I'm not sure I ever would have appreciated a moment like that, nor would I ever have considered the possibility that there could be a day when I'd long for something so simple. Our lives had been full and busy. Our phones were always nearby—mine was almost always in my hand. Moments sped past as we lived our lives. Now, we were *here*, forced to slow down; forced to learn to wait; forced to live in moments of yearning. Only then were we blessed with the rewards for our patience. This—the rewriting of our future love story—was one of the greatest blessings God had bestowed on us throughout this awful experience. He had given me an opportunity to stop offering a watered down, finite version of love and had taught me what that word really meant. Here in Charlie's room, our flesh finally meeting, that powerful, heart-pounding love was growing faster than I'd ever dreamed it could.

Over the next few days, I worked to make Charlie's room comfortable. First, I hung the three pictures of the boys right in front of her bed where she could easily see them. Then, finally allowed to hang cards, I got to work hanging as many as I could on a single wall so they were visible but not overwhelming the room. Next, I arranged flowers from our wonderful community members; I placed them on the windowsill, nightstand, and even on the tray over Charlie's bed. I made sure her mini-fridge was stocked with all her favorite drinks, including chocolate protein shakes, 7-Up, and of course, sweet tea.

When the last cards were hung and the final flower arrangement placed, I pulled up a chair next to Charlie's bed and poured us each a 7-Up. We clinked our plastic glasses and relaxed for a moment, basking in this new environment that felt a little like home. I looked at Charlie and put my hand on hers. As she stared back at me, there was something unmissable in her eyes. Where there was once fear and sadness, there was something else, and it wasn't just hope. For the first time, I saw in Charlies eyes a deep knowing that everything was going to be all right.

I felt overwhelmed with emotions of fear, and this thought that Charlie did not survive the accident, I know that I am not even close to be done processing this incredible life changing event/trauma that Charlie and our family has experienced. I had a very hard time staying asleep last night, because my mind kept racing in different directions, I pray that tonight I am able to have a better night of sleep.

Excerpt from Journal, February 18, 2022

CHAPTER 28

Evidence

The headlights of my car illuminated the garage doors as I pulled into the driveway. I turned off the ignition, gathered my things and, as though on autopilot, I jumped out of the car and headed toward the house. Although winter was wearing on me, I loved seeing the house all lit up in the dark. It represented consistent warmth and comfort at a time when I needed it most. The only thing it lacked, however, was Charlie's beautiful presence.

As I approached the door, I noticed a large box on the landing. At first, I thought it must be from Amazon, Charlie often shopped for the boys from her iPad, but as I got closer, I noticed the box was plain and tattered. I nudged it with my foot to get it out of the way of the door and noticed then just how heavy it was. I lugged the box into the house and placed it on my desk, then went about my evening playing with the boys, feeding them dinner, and getting them tucked into bed.

Later that evening when the house was quiet and dim, I walked into my office and grabbed a letter opener. I quickly sliced through the tape on the box and pried the top open before peeking inside. There, staring back at me, was a black bag with a yellow tag on it marked "evidence."

My stomach lurched.

My heart raced.

I reached down to touch it. My hand grazed metal. I tore open the bag. Inside was the melted, gnarled sander Charlie had been using on the morning of the accident, along with the extension cords it had been plugged into.

I had been so conscious of remaining in a place of gratitude that I wasn't prepared for the feelings that were flooding my body. Tears filled my eyes and splashed down into the box. I backed away slowly, my hands covering my face. I sank to the floor.

For the first time in a long time, my mind flashed through all the *what ifs* I'd so rarely let myself think about.

Our sons sobbed for Mommy.

There was no glossing of the truth—we couldn't explain it away as a "boo-boo."

I was standing in front of our loved ones.

I was delivering a eulogy.

There was no more joy.

There was no more hope.

There was only sadness.

There was only pain.

I opened my eyes, stood, and stared back down into the box. There, next to the sander, in the darkness deep within the cardboard, I saw a life without Charlie.

That night, I tossed and turned. I begged sleep to come, to carry me from the thoughts I couldn't shake, but I remained in a space of utter despair; it was somewhere I hadn't been in so long. I kept thing back to my first night in bed without Charlie. How cold her side of the bed felt; how I felt I could reach into the darkness eternally, searching for her. Even though I *knew* Charlie was beating all odds, living an incredible story of recovery and rehabilitation, my body was catapulted backward. As night faded into dawn, sleep eluded me, leaving me to suffer beneath the weight of knowing the depths of suffering we so narrowly missed.

Today we had a very special conversation with one of Charlie's favorite nurses, it is just surreal to hear from others on how close Charlie really got to death, one day I hope I can share the content of this conversation that had all three of us crying, I am so grateful for her nurses, they are incredible humans, and we are so happy to be getting to know them. After that conversation Charlie and I just looked at each other in disbelief and we are so grateful for her life! We are very aware of the miracle of Charlie's life and recovery!

—Excerpt from Journal Entry, January 19, 2022

CHAPTER 29

The Heart of Healing

Alarms screamed. The shrill, piercing sound echoed off the walls, bouncing back and forth down the long, hollow hallway. Doctors' and nurses' shoes squeaked on the tile as they flew by, racing to the room next-door. I reached out and grabbed Charlie's hand. We knew what these sounds meant—someone had gone code blue. I squeezed her hand against my palm as the volume increased. Additional alarms began to sound as nurses and doctors shouted over one another.

"Quickly, don't stop!"

"Try harder!"

"We're losing him!"

"Get the **Dopamine**! MORE **DOPAMINE**!"

"STAY WITH US!"

Charlie closed her eyes as the shouting slowed to a stop and, one by one, the machines' shrill screams stopped. I kissed Charlie's head and walked to the doorway, watching as doctors and nurses exited the room. One nurse put her hand on another nurse's back. They both knelt to the ground, trying to stifle sobs, comforting one another as the truth began to settle in: they had lost someone. It wouldn't be the first time, nor would it be the last. Sadly, a lot of death happened in that room.

The room next to Charlie's was one that held unbelievable darkness and pain. I learned something from spending so much time in the Burn Unit; something I'd never heard of: self-immolation. This term refers to the act of lighting oneself on fire, typically in an attempt to commit suicide. Previously unfamiliar to me, the term was now permanently imprinted on my mind. The room right next to Charlie's was where they would bring those who attempted to die by self-immolation. Over Charlie's time in the unit, four separate people came in after suicide attempts. All of them later passed away. These were moments of deep mourning for the staff. As some of them broke down together and others walked slowly down the hallway, grief-stricken, I wanted to come out of Charlie's room and offer them comfort. I wanted to hold their hands, talk with them, and show them the same type of love they had always shown Charlie. Instead, I hung back and offered a silent prayer of gratitude for the huge personal investment made by every staff member at the hospital. They consistently showed compassion and love beyond measure. Their incredible work was a steady reminder of the human side of healthcare.

Of course, I will not pretend that the American healthcare system isn't difficult—if not impossible—to deal with at times. There are politics to navigate, rules to follow, and standards of care to contend with. Knowing this, I entered the hospital as Charlie's advocate expecting to experience opposition at every turn. At first, I was short with the staff, even hard on them, mostly in anticipation of doctors and nurses making poor decisions about Charlie's care. I waited to see nurses rush around, treating her coldly, performing their jobs like she was just another part of a day's work. I put up my fists. I waited for the villains to come. But they never did. Instead, what I found was kindness and compassion, care and concern, and beautiful, selfless acts of love from doctors and nurses whose passion was palpable.

I will never forget the first time I sat in my chair and stared across the room at Charlie, watching her receive one of the most tender acts of kindness. Her eyes were closed, and her face was completely relaxed as her chest rose and fell. Behind Charlie was her nurse, Olivia, who had come in an hour earlier with a surprise. She was holding a bowl of warm water, an absorbent pad, and a small bottle of shampoo. She slid the pad beneath Charlie's head and began slowly trickling the water over her scalp, then squeezed shampoo into her hands, and started massaging her head, working the soap into a lather. From my vantage point, I could see every muscle in Charlie's body relax as she let the feeling of ecstasy drape over her like a warm, weighted blanket.

This was the essence of Olivia—pure, unconditional love.

Olivia was a travelling nurse who had a contract with VCU. She was quickly assigned to Charlie's case, becoming one of her first nurses in the burn ICU. Right from the beginning, it was clear that Olivia was special. Although all the nurses were fantastic, gently offering comfort and vigilant monitoring, Olivia did so with extra care and compassion.

As time passed, Olivia became the master of going above and beyond in her care for Charlie. In those very first weeks when she was intubated and desperate for water, Olivia came up with a solution that gave her some relief without risking her health and safety. Olivia would get a cup of ice water and a tool the size of a Q-tip with a sponge at the very end. She would sit by Charlie's side, dip the sponge in the water, and run it along Charlie's lips and tongue, just to give her the sensation of moisture in her mouth. Charlie would desperately suck on the sponge and then release it for Olivia to dip back into the water and repeat the process to quell Charlie's desperation. I remember watching as her face relaxed while Olivia ran her fingers over Charlie's forehead as she received the tiny droplets of water. I could hardly believe the way this one act brought such comfort and calm to Charlie who was living with such torturous, unrelenting thirst.

In time, I felt myself softening to all the people who were providing Charlie's care. Not only did the nurses create a feeling of safety and comfort, but the doctors and surgeons did too. I was hard on that team. I pushed Dr. Bergin and Charlie's other doctors. When things seemed to be going sideways, I would find them in the hallways, request meetings, and do anything I could to get them to listen to me, to hear about the research I had done, and to understand what I believed were the right next steps. As frustrated as I became at times, I had to admit that I was never ignored. Dr. Bergin and his team consistently made time, listened, and met my concerns with honest opinions and straightforward answers. The team never shut me down, nor did they make me feel like I wasn't worthy of their time. In fact, they always made sure to compliment me on the research I'd done and my devotion to Charlie. Knowing that they were open to hearing what I had to say was a beautiful gift. I no longer sat on pins and needles waiting for someone to do something awful. I was no longer poised, expecting someone to drop the ball. Instead, I looked around and saw a team of people desperately working together to heal the love of my life. Together, they hadn't just saved her. They'd worked with Charlie and her body's miraculous rebound, offering care that sped her healing up tremendously.

Looking back, I so clearly see the role the staff at VCU played in my personal evolution. Previously, I was someone who saw kindness as a bargaining chip—something that was unnecessary unless it was being paid back in some way. Yet, as I watched this team of incredible people work miracles while showing such sensitivity and empathy, I learned what kindness really is.

Kindness is love.

I apologize to him, for the few times that I made demands and argued with him, he also complemented both of us, for the love towards each other and for my fighting spirit to protect and advocate for my wife

—Excerpt from Journal Entry, February 25, 2022

CHAPTER 30

No Kids Allowed

I could hardly believe it, but the time had come. I was packing up Charlie's room and getting her prepared for her move to Sheltering Arms rehabilitation. With every photo I took off the walls, every card I placed on the pile, and every vase I cleaned out, I reflected on the time Charlie had spent in the hospital. There was that first day when I raced to her side, the first moments when I thought I was going to lose her, the fear of infection, the arguments over her care plan, the legal drama, and the pain Charlie endured. But there were also the miracles. The moments when grafts took better than expected, the times when Charlie came through infections unscathed, the moments when all hope should be lost, but instead, it was found. So much had happened within the walls of this hospital, it was surprisingly emotional to say goodbye.

Two days before Charlie was scheduled to go to rehab, just as I got into my car in the hospital parking lot, my phone rang. "Hello?" I answered, placing the pile of cards I'd been holding on the passenger seat.

"Mr. Xavier, this is Sharon from Sheltering Arms, how are you?"

"I'm well, thank you. We're looking forward to Charlie's transfer this week."

"We're looking forward to it too," she responded, "but I do have one thing to discuss with you."

"Sure," I said, now backing out of my spot.

"I know we had previously discussed your sons being able to visit Charlie while she is at Sheltering Arms. Unfortunately, due to our increasing measures to prevent COVID-19 outbreaks here at the facility, we are not allowing children to visit at this time."

"Wait, wait, wait. What?"

"I'm sorry, I know this is hard news, but—"

"No, this will be devastating to Charlie. She's been working toward being able to see her sons. This isn't acceptable."

"I wish there was something I could do."

"Well, is there anything at all you can do?"

"Unfortunately, not. I'm so sorry, Mr. Xavier."

I leaned forward and tapped the button to end the call on my car's Bluetooth system. I didn't know what to think or do. My heart began to pound, my thoughts began to race. I wondered if I could get Charlie into another facility on such short notice, but I knew it wouldn't be possible. I imagined her face when I told her that she wouldn't be able to see the boys while she was at rehab. I imagined her eyes filling with tears. I imagined her losing hope.

I should have known better.

The next day, I sat next to Charlie and cautiously delivered the news. "Charlie," I started, "we have a problem. I spoke with Sheltering Arms yesterday and they are not going to allow the boys to visit you while you're there."

She stared back at me.

"Listen, all hope is not lost. The way I see it, we have three options. One, we will complain; make a lot of noise. I will contact colleagues and other people we know in the media and do an interview to put pressure on Sheltering Arms. Two, I'll reach out to our friend at the governor's office and …"

"What are you doing?" Charlie asked, a quizzical look on her face.

"I'm sorry?" I asked, puzzled.

"Who do you think you are? We're not special. We can't just have people bend rules for us. Of course, I'm disappointed, but we're not entitled to different treatment just because we're connected."

I sat back in my chair, unsure of what to say next. Every ounce of me wanted to fight, to find a way around this injustice that was being done to Charlie. She had worked so hard—been through so much—and she was finally getting to leave. Part of the thrill was that she'd be able to reconnect with the boys, hold them in her arms, make up for lost time. Now, that had been taken from her and she didn't even want to fight it. There was no part of me that understood why Charlie would ask me to sit back and allow Sheltering Arms to take something so vital away from our family.

Not wanting to argue, I stood up and walked out of the room and into the hallway. I sat down in a chair nearby and held my head in my hands. I had been fighting for Charlie, advocating for her for so long, that I couldn't imagine not fighting for her now, especially when the stakes were so high. I felt frustrated. I felt shamed. Then it came, a familiar feeling—deep, cutting anger. My face hot, I wanted to stand up, stomp back into Charlie's room, and start yelling. I wanted to force her to see my perspective. I wanted to make her see things my way so that, together, we could fight through this just like we fought through everything else. I clenched my fists and closed my eyes tightly. I felt like I could explode.

Then I took a breath.

And another.

And another.

And another.

My shoulders dropped, I unclenched my fists, and I opened my eyes. To my surprise, the anger had vanished. It was as if my body was no longer a hospitable environment for that emotion. Instead, I let myself breathe and think. Did I want Charlie to understand my perspective? Of course. Did I wish that she would let me fight for her—for our family? Yes. But this journey was one that Charlie ultimately needed to guide. It was my responsibility to love and support her. I had to put my own feelings aside for the time being.

I let myself linger in the hallway a little longer, watching as nurses crossed from room to room, listening to the soft hum of machines. In that moment, I drew a breath and allowed myself to feel gratitude. We were a family that came into the healthcare system with a great understanding of the way business works. And hospitals, though places of healing, are also businesses. Without our shared understanding of the way businesses operate, I'm not sure Charlie and I would have been able to navigate the system as smoothly as we had thus far. The key word there is *navigate*; the path was not cut and dry. Together, Charlie and I worked within the confines that were presented to us. We pushed when we had to, we let things flow when it was the right thing to do, and we fought hard when circumstances called for it. We did not, however, feel entitled because of our standing within the community. We never expected more than we were so graciously being given. We would not be commanding, demanding, or forceful. Instead, we would be grateful and accepting of our circumstances, even if they weren't exactly as we'd hoped. That, I realized, was the crux of Charlie's frustration with my desire to fight this new policy. She saw me contemplating stepping over the line in the sand we had drawn; she called me on it.

I stood from the chair and walked back to Charlie's room. As soon as I walked through the door, I could tell she expected me to return angry and ready for a fight. The André from *before* would have come into the room ready for a shouting match. This André was too grateful and far too full of love to be dragged down by something that, in the long run, would seem so small.

I crossed the floor and sat in the chair next to Charlie's bed. I reached out for her hand, held it in mine, and gave it a kiss. "I'm sorry," I said quietly. "Please know, I was coming from a place of love. My first instinct is always to fight for you."

"I love that about you, Babe. But, this time, you don't have to."

[Today was] the day we dreamed about, and it was just amazing to see [Charlie] leaving the hospital after almost six months! It was a day filled with emotions, lots of gratitude, happiness, a little fear, nervousness, all mixed together, as I write this post, I am emotionally drained.

I do feel a huge sense of accomplishment for Charlie, she has overcome the first chapter of this life long Journey, yes Charlie Journey has truly just started, now we embark on the second chapter, in my opinion a more difficult one, and you may wonder , how can it be more difficult than fighting to stay alive, well her fight now is with herself and pain, she has an incredible adversary to face, herself.

—Excerpt from Journal Entry, March 1, 2022

CHAPTER 31

Exit

As the sun went down, I packed the last of Charlie's things into boxes. There were still piles and piles of cards, big framed photos, her mini-fridge, and other items that had made her room feel like home. Now, with everything piled up near the door, the room had returned to its old, lifeless form, which was all well and good. The next morning, Charlie would be leaving the hospital for Sheltering Arms.

Before I left for the night, Charlie and I took a quiet moment together. I stared at her, taking in her radiant smile, her big, sparkling eyes, her essence. I could hardly believe the changes that had occurred since the accident and how our relationship had strengthened. I felt such intense love for my wife, I barely knew what to do with the feelings. Our relationship was no longer simple. It was now complex, layered, nearly dizzying in its depths.

I leaned forward and kissed her on the lips, "I'll see you tomorrow, my love."

She looked up at me, reached up, and placed her hand on my face. "Tomorrow," she whispered. "I love you."

The next morning, when I arrived at the hospital with my mom and the boys, we walked quickly through the parking lot. The early spring air was chilly, ruffling the boys' hair as we rushed toward the ambulance bay. Weeks prior, I'd set up an exclusive with a local news station so they'd be the one and only network to cover the exact moment when Charlie left the hospital and was placed into an ambulance and taken to rehab. The camera crew was already there and set up when we finally got to the doors.

As we stood, shifting from foot to foot as we anticipated Charlie's bed rolling through the doors, London pulled on my arm. "Daddy, I'm cold. Can you get my jacket?"

"London, we're waiting for Mommy."

"But I'm cold."

"We're waiting to see Mommy."

"Please?"

"Fine," I sighed, "Mom, will you make sure you have an eye on London? I have to run to the car."

With that, I took off running toward our car, which we'd parked much farther away than I'd wanted to. I sprinted past car after car before tapping the button on my key fob to open my trunk. I ran to the car, grabbed London's jacket, pushed the button to close it again, and dashed back to the hospital. Once I finally had the ambulance bay in sight, it had erupted with cheers. Charlie had already come out! I ran to her side with London's jacket tucked beneath my arms.

This was the first time since the accident that Charlie and the kids were getting to see one another in person. London asked to be picked up so he could give her a big hug. Once we put London back on the ground, I took Julien from my mom and tried to hand him to Charlie. He buried his head in my shoulder, refusing to look at her. I could see the pain in Charlie's eyes, but there was no time to dwell, we had to head to Sheltering Arms. As the EMS crew loaded Charlie into the ambulance, I let them know that I'd be right behind them and would meet them there.

When we arrived at the rehab facility, a huge group of Charlie's friends, around 25 of then, were already gathered. They were all in clown costumes doing cartwheels, cheering, and applauding. They were all holding orchids (Charlie's favorite) and big bunches of balloons. There was no sign of the ambulance yet, so we joined the jubilant group to wait.

As time ticked by and Charlie's friends continued to cheer and shout excitedly, an administrator came out to talk to me.

"I'm sorry, but this has to stop," she said. "There are so many people, and a camera crew? It's too much for right outside the facility. We don't want to upset patients or cause too much of a disturbance."

I suppressed my frustration and said, "I promise, we won't be here much longer. We just want to see Charlie arrive. Can you find out where she is?"

"Mr. Xavier, she's already here. The ambulance arrives at a back entrance."

My face fell, "Oh my God, please. Is there anything you can do? We've been waiting to see her."

She smiled slyly and nodded.

Moments later, Charlie was wheeled on a stretcher out the front door so everyone could welcome her. Friends jumped and screamed, blew horns, and danced. London was able to give her one more hug and Julien even let himself be placed on Charlie's lap. I walked over and gave Charlie a kiss then whispered, "I'm just going to say goodbye to everyone, then I'll be right in."

"Okay," she nodded, clinging to my arm until she was wheeled away.

CHAPTER 32

Little Girl Alone

Once everyone was gone and my mom had taken the boys home, I was ready to go inside and help get Charlie set up in her new room. Recalling how pristine the rooms were, I knew I could add a few touches to make it feel like home easily, especially with the orchids and balloons her friends brought.

My hands full of flowers and balloons, I clumsily pulled my mask over my mouth and nose as I walked into the lobby. I nodded to the receptionist who looked up from her computer and immediately waved me over. She raised her eyebrows and said, "I'm sorry, but those flowers aren't permitted in the facility."

"What do you mean? Why can't I bring flowers in?" I asked.

"The only flowers we allow are fresh cut ones in water. We can't have dirt brought inside, it's not sanitary."

"Are you serious?" I responded. I could feel my cheeks flush.

"Unfortunately, yes. I can hold them for you," she offered, "but they can't be brought farther than this point."

I had to remind myself to breathe deeply as I felt white hot anger burning inside me. "Please?" I begged, "My wife has been through so much and we only just learned that we can't bring our boys to see her. If you'll just let me—"

"I'm sorry, I wish I could, but I just can't," she replied.

I stared back at her, drew a breath, and reminded myself of Charlie's words: *we're not special.* I choked back tears as I placed the pots on the receptionist's desk, promising I'd save the fight for something much bigger.

By 8:30 p.m., the sky had gone from dusty pink to pitch black with big, fat stars strewn across it. I had set up Charlie's mini-fridge and filled it with her favorite drinks. I hung the big pictures of the boys and placed other framed photos all over the room. I'd also arranged the few bunches of fresh cut flowers we'd received and made sure Charlie was comfortable with plush blankets and pillows from home. I glanced at my watch. Visiting hours had technically ended thirty-minutes earlier. "Shoot. I need to go now, honey."

I looked up to see Charlie staring over at me from her bed. Her eyes were wide and glassy, her bottom lip quivered. "Please don't leave me here," she pleaded in a whisper.

"I'll be back tomorrow," I said, kneeling next to her.

"I know, but I'm scared. I'm so scared. I don't want to be here alone."

"Honey, I'm sorry, but I have to—"

"Just please, please stay?" she begged. "Please?"

Tears rolled down her face, wetting the sheets she'd pulled up to her chin. I sat down on the bed next to her and held her hand, suddenly understanding what was behind the fear. In the hustle and bustle of getting her ready to leave VCU, I'd forgotten that the hospital had become home to Charlie. There, she had her routine. She knew her nurses and doctors well. She trusted the staff. She knew they would care for her with love and respect. Now, in this cavernous room in a building she'd never been inside, the unknown loomed.

"I know you're afraid. It's scary being in a new place, especially after being at the hospital for so long. The thing is, you have to try hard to remember that this is just another step, and it's a required one. You have to get through this to get home to us," I said, leaning into her.

She nodded.

"Now, it's about the mental fight to push yourself through this big step, right?"

She nodded again then replied, "I know, but the pain is going to be so awful. I just know it. I'm scared I can't do it."

"Charlie," I said, carefully placing my hand on her knee, "think about how far you've come. You've experienced so much pain already; you *can* do this. You are so strong."

I picked up her hand once more and began to pray. I asked God for comfort and peace. I begged Him to watch over Charlie and asked him to take her pain. I asked Him to watch over her this night and always.

Once I finished the prayer, we sat together in silence. I let my mind wander, allowing myself to think about the entire expanse of our experience. For a moment, I let my mind wander to *before.* I thought about our family brunches, laughing together over mimosas, playing with the kids. I thought about our time together dreaming up our businesses, specifically Patch and how excited Charlie was. I wondered what life could have been without the spark that engulfed my wife and stole so much. It was something I would never know, but in that moment, all I wanted to do was go back, even just for one moment. I lay my head on the pillow next to Charlie's and listened as she broke down. She let herself cry about not being able to see the boys while she was there. She allowed herself to talk about the pain. She let herself grieve her body, her old life, things that once felt simple that now felt impossible.

For the next hour, Charlie continued to sob silently, her shoulders rising and falling as she tried to catch her breath. I willed myself to stay calm as I comforted her, but soon tears were pricking the backs of my eyes too. I wanted to hold her all night. I wanted to stay there forever. I wanted to cradle her in my arms and promise never to let go. But I couldn't make promises that I knew would be broken. I had to fight to be strong.

"Honey, I love you," I said, "I know you're so scared, but you are safe here, I promise. I'll be back tomorrow as early as I can possibly get here."

She nodded her head, pressing her lips together to prevent sobs from escaping.

"You can do this. I promise you. I love you so much." I stood, bent down and gave her a long, lingering kiss. I held her face. The light from her side table caught the glistening tears in her eyes. "I love you," I repeated, then I headed to the door. Before I left, I glanced over my shoulder for one last look at her. Yet, there, in the dim light, I could no longer see my wife. All I saw was a little girl—alone.

I couldn't help but squint my eyes as the bright light of the hallway struck me. My shoes squeaked on the tile floor as I made my way to the elevator. My heart was pounding, my breath was quick. I needed to get outside before I turned around and ran back to Charlie's side. Leaving her like that had shattered my heart.

My walk to the elevator felt endless. My throat was tight, my cheeks and eyes ached from the tears I had wiped away. Six months ago, I never could have envisioned even walking into a place like this. Now, here I was, about to exit the building with my wife still inside. Once I finally reached the elevator bay, I pressed the button several times, willing it to get there fast. As I looked back down the hallway, I thought about the people in each room I had passed. I wondered what they'd been through, and what they continued to go through. I wondered how many family members and loved ones had made this very same walk to the elevator and waited in this spot, holding their breath as they left. I wondered how many people had experienced the kind of breakdown Charlie and I had just shared and how they managed to pull themselves away. I wondered if some of them couldn't make themselves leave and had to be escorted out. *I wondered.*

Once the elevator finally arrived, I stepped inside. I leaned against the wall and adjusted my mask, ready to yank it off as soon as I could. When the elevator hit the ground floor, I jogged through reception, bursting through the doors to the parking lot and tore the mask from my face. The cool night air filled my lungs as I stood beneath a streetlight and let myself burst into tears. There was so much emotion inside me—so much sadness, pain, and anger that I couldn't contain it. It was spilling out everywhere and all I wanted was to go home with Charlie. I wanted her to stand up, walk out of her room, shed her scars, and make her way to the car with me. I wanted to drive to our house which would be lit and warm, welcoming us as we walked up the front stairs to the door. I wanted to walk inside and be greeted by the boys who would scream and shout that Mommy was home. I wanted to be in our room together. I wanted to sleep with her in my arms. I yearned for all these things—things that might never be.

When the tears finally subsided, I turned to face the building. There, overlooking the parking lot, was a wall of glass. I stepped forward to look through it, my eyes scanning the massive gym. The bright lights illuminated each piece of equipment, glinting off the metal, casting an ethereal glow over the lawn outside. As my eyes scanned the machines, I let myself take in the moment. Charlie had come so far and, although this place represented healing, it also represented the losses that needed to be regained. There was the place where she'd stretch, the place where she'd work on rebuilding strength in her arms, and the place where she'd work on mobility. That's when my eyes fell on it: a wheelchair. Then, shockingly, for the first time since the accident, it dawned on me that Charlie may never walk again.

I stepped back as this thought took root in my mind. I'd been head down, so focused on Charlie's healing and recovery that I never stopped to think about what our end point might actually look like. All this time, I'd imagined Charlie coming home and returning to some semblance of the life we knew. Yet, this wheelchair reminded me that our lives might very well be changed in a drastic way. Not just now, but *forever*. My throat tightened. I took a breath and pulled myself back to center.

Charlie's healing has been miraculous.

Charlie will continue to fight.

Charlie is alive.

I will be by her side, always.

I am grateful.

I am grateful.

I am grateful.

I stepped backwards away from the building and turned toward my car. As I left the stream of light that poured from the gym, the night air swirled around me. I looked up at the stars and reminded myself that without darkness, there is no light.

"Today we talked about so many things, but at one point our conversation became very emotional and Charlie shared some raw feelings with me, she talked about some of her thoughts in regards to her new body, I was so proud of her to have the courage to be vulnerable with me. It was very emotional and raw. We talked about, how when time is right, she will have to grief the loss of her previous body and life, she has the right to do so, her healing is just starting, her new skin will need up to 18 months to fully heal, but Only God knows how long her mind and soul will take to be healed, but the most important step she already took, she is grateful to be alive. [Together, we are] starting to embrace vulnerability."

—**Excerpt from Journal Entry, January 20, 2022**

.

Afterword

Three weeks before the accident, Charlie stood in the kitchen with her arms crossed. "I don't understand why you act that way toward him," she said, her brows knitted together.

"Charlie, I'm his father. That means my job is to help him become a strong man."

"A *strong man?*" she repeated. "I don't know what your definition of a strong man is but treating him that way is not doing anything good for your relationship with him. He cried himself to sleep."

"All he does is complain. I'm not going to stand there and watch him cry like a baby over toothpaste."

"He's five. He *is* a baby. You can't be so hard on him."

"I'm going to be hard on him until he becomes a *man.*"

"Why are you like this? I don't understand." She stared deep into my eyes as tears formed in the corners of hers.

I shook my head and rolled my eyes.

Just then, my mind flashed back to when I was a small child. I'd fallen and scraped my knee and ran into my house crying. My dad took one look at me, raised his hand, and slammed it down on my backside. *I'll give you something to cry about!* He bellowed.

I broke eye contact with Charlie and looked down at my phone, "I have work to do."

She stormed out of the kitchen, frustrated.

I tried not to think about it, but the thoughts swept me away. I had spent my entire childhood fearful of my father. He was hard and unfeeling. His punishments were swift and harsh. His words cut like glass. And although Charlie knew parts of that, she would never know how it made me feel. She would also never know that, for a moment—one tiny, microscopic moment—I felt sad that I didn't know how to be a better father than my dad had been to me. Charlie would never know because she didn't need to know. That information was unnecessary to share. I believed there was absolutely no value in vulnerability. To be vulnerable was to be weak.

When I started Charlie's Survival Journal, I never stopped to think about what it would become. At first I was just looking for an easy way to keep everyone updated on Charlie's condition and to build a community that would support her as she fought for her life. I made it a priority to keep the journal up-to-date and made sure that writing was a part of my daily routine. No matter what my day was like, how hard things had been, or how exhausted I was, as soon as the boys were asleep, I'd sit in my office or sprawl out on my bed and write a long update on my phone. Sometimes, my fingers would fly as I expressed gratitude, shared exciting updates, and related pieces of good news. Other times, I'd have to fight through tears to get the words out, and as soon as I was finished, I'd curl into a ball on Charlie's side of the bed and cry myself to sleep. No matter what, I'd wake to hundreds of messages of support, love, and promises of prayers. Oftentimes, the kindness and encouragement I received from the community members was the thing that got me out of bed in the morning. It didn't matter what was happening or how I was feeling, the support I received showed me just how much love there is in the world. And that love changed me.

Soon what began as a place to share facts about what was going on in our lives, became a place where I found something I'd been missing my whole life: the ability to be vulnerable. I was learning just how wrong I'd been. Vulnerability wasn't weakness; it was the pathway to strength and gratitude. The online journal became a place for me to open up and share everything I was experiencing as I advocated for Charlie; my fears, my concerns, my deepest thoughts and desires. The more I shared, the more readers shared back. The more raw, honest, and open I became, the bigger the group grew. I found myself softening, listening, and holding honest conversations with friends and followers in front of thousands of eager readers. The version of me that existed before Charlie's horrific accident would rarely, if ever, listen and share back. Yet, I was beginning to see how vital it was to my mental and emotional stability to open myself up, to build community, to accept help, love, and support. With this came deep gratitude. Not just for me, but for Charlie too.

Of course, Charlie and I will always have moments—even days or weeks—when we feel the sting of grief. We look back at the time *before* when life was simple, and we excitedly planned the future. And even though it's easy to idealize *then*, things are so much clearer now. The arguments that Charlie and I had were intense and it pains me to say that many of them were caused by me, my issues, and my ego. I couldn't even loosen the grip on my ego for long enough to make a single change. I was hard hearted, strong-willed, and stubborn. I look back at that version of me and see so clearly what was going on. It was a time before I knew what the word *love* really meant.

As much as we all—especially Charlie—lost on the day of the accident, we feel an overwhelming sense of gratitude for the things we did not lose and for the things we gained. The most important thing is that Charlie survived. That is where our blessings began. From that point forward, Charlie beat every one of the odds she was up against. She pushed herself through some of the most painful procedures one can go through, and she often did so with a smile on her face. Today, she continues to build incredible strength as we once again look into the future with hope.

Standing by Charlie's side, I have learned so much about myself, my place in the world, and the man I want to be. On the day of the accident, it was as if my life was a puzzle pulled apart, put back in its box, and shaken. I entered this experience as a person with a cold, hard heart and, over time, have felt myself soften. I have learned that my ego won't get me far in life whereas kindness and compassion create infinite opportunities for happiness beyond measure. The road ahead might not be smooth, but it is open, beckoning us to continue. With a humble heart I will forge ahead by Charlie's side, offering love and the best care possible as she continues to fight.

Together, Charlie and I look ahead at what's next and marvel at how far we've come. Charlie went from a three percent chance of survival and the likelihood of a minimum of one year in the hospital to home before the one-year anniversary of the accident. As she continues to recover, we have good days and bad days. Slowly, Charlie is learning to deal with her level of mobility and to fully recognize how hard and far she can push herself. We are working on ideas of how we can give it back, since we have received so much. We know that God has a plan, and we already know that giving is part of that plan. As I continue my role of Advocate as she continues to recover from home. We stand united as we forge ahead. Today and always, Charlie and I remain focused on God, His blessings, and all that He has in store for us.

Acknowledgments

As I reflect on the last 12 months, It is hard to believe that we have come so far, it is also hard not to think about the people that helped us along this impossible journey, my mother, Maria das Graças and her unconditional love, my sister Marianna and her fiancée Giulliano. They dropped their lives in Brazil and came to our rescue. They helped me with the boys for a few months until they had to return to their lives, also grateful for Charlie's Family support.

We are eternally grateful to our friends for stepping up in full force and providing us with meals, childcare, love and support. Your actions have been a significant inspiration for me. You have shown me how amazing it is to give. I now know the joy that giving provides.

I am forever grateful to my friend and business partner Jon. He witnessed the accident and helped Charlie by calling 911, then calling me. Jon did not hesitate to step in and fill my gap during the months that I couldn't work. His parents, Bill and Wendy, have also been amazing to our family and have worked so hard to make Patch Brewing Co. a successful business. I am forever grateful for all your support and help.

I am grateful for the heroic effort during Charlie's rescue from the Gordonsville Volunteer Fire Company.

The Medical Team at VCU Health Evans-Haynes Burn Center, and the Sheltering Arms, Sheltering Arms Institute: Physical Rehabilitation Hospital for their professionalism and care.

I am forever grateful for the thousands of cards, messages, donations, and prayers we received from people worldwide. Charlie's healing journey would have been far more painful without you all.

To our sons London and Julien, I want you to know that you both are the reason why your mother survived; her love for you gave her the strength to survive the impossible. We love you beyond your imagination, I am proud of the man you will become.

Lastly, I would like to thank you, Charlie, you are the love of my life, and I am so honored to be by your side; during the most challenging moments of our lives, our love just became stronger, and your strength humbled me! You inspire me daily!

Made in the USA
Monee, IL
21 September 2022

14399223R00148